Women
and
Jesus

Women
and
Jesus

Alicia Craig Faxon

A Pilgrim Press Book
from
United Church Press
Philadelphia

Library of Congress Cataloging in Publication Data

Faxon, Alicia Craig.
    Women and Jesus.
    "A Pilgrim Press book."
    Bibliography: p.
    1. Jesus Christ—Attitude towards women. 2. Women
in the Bible. I. Title.
BT590.W6F38   225.8'30141'2   72–11868
ISBN 0–8298–0244–4

United Church Press, 1505 Race Street,
Philadelphia, Pennsylvania 19102

Contents

Introduction

There is no question that one of the foremost issues of the 1970's is the issue of women's liberation. The communications media have exposed it in its more dramatic manifestations, and numerous studies, articles, and books on the rights of women have been appearing in ever-increasing number. Some commentators see women's liberation as the most significant question of this decade while others go further to say that the world's principal modern problem is the suppression of women economically, politically, intellectually, socially, and spiritually.

These commentators are not impassioned latter-day suffragettes looking for a new cause but are thoughtful men and women seeing the signs of cultural malaise on all sides. Women have been in the forefront in calling attention to the problem. Betty Friedan's *The Feminine Mystique*, appearing in the early 1960's, was perhaps the clarion call of the movement and was followed shortly by Caroline Bird's *Born Female: The High Cost of Keeping Women Down*, which explored the economic implications of the suppression of women. In 1970 Kate Millett's *Sexual Politics* completed the trilogy, taking the question into the realm of politics. It was in the area of political life that Shirley Chisholm continued the fight, making the memorable statement in a press conference that during her life as a Black and as a woman, she had been discriminated against more as a woman than as a Black.

Since then numerous anthologies of studies and articles on different aspects of women's liberation have appeared, clearly testifying to a widespread interest and concern about the role of women. Many institutions of society are being examined in the light of their relation to women in today's world.

The Christian church has become the focus for some searching questions on its teachings, organization, and missionary outreach to women. Probing books such as *Women's Liberation and the Church*, edited by Sarah Bentley Doley, *The Church and the Second Sex* by Dr. Mary Daly of Boston College, and *The Illusion of Eve* by Sidney Callahan have examined the role of women in both the Protestant and Roman churches. They have pointed out with justice that the church has tended to follow the culture rather than lead it, and many pronouncements and assumptions about "woman's place" in the church have put her in the role of a second-class citizen in the kingdom. Many churches have become concerned with equality for minority groups such as Blacks, Puerto Ricans, ghetto-dwellers, migrant workers, etc., but the religious establishment in general has not seriously considered the problem of equal rights for women either in society or in ecclesiastical structures.

There are signs of concern about civil rights for women shown by the Roman Catholic Church in its statement from Vatican II, *The Pastoral Constitution on the Church in the Modern World* (n.29) which states:

> With respect to the fundamental rights of the person, every type of discrimination, whether social or cultural, whether based on sex, race, color, social condition, language or religion, is to be overcome and eradicated as contrary to God's intent. For in truth it must still be regretted that fundamental personal rights are not yet being universally honored. Such is the case of a woman who is denied the right and freedom to choose a husband, to embrace a style of life, or to acquire an education or cultural benefits equal to those recognized for men.

In Protestant churches there is also a movement toward a greater realization of the potential of women and a greater utilization of their talents in the world and within the organization of the church.

For example, in the Episcopal Church women have recently been elected to serve on the vestry, the governing body of the individual parish. Women also are now eligible to serve as delegates to the General Convention, which is the main governing body of the Episcopal Church in the United States. Women are being ordained in many branches of the Protestant church, although their actual areas of service are often circumscribed by the prejudices of congregations against having a woman preach or take a leading executive position in the church. Too often women are shunted to jobs dealing with the education of children or special "women's ministry," regardless of their inclinations, talents, or training.

This is a serious reflection on the nature of the Christian church. If the Lord our God is presented as a righteous God and yet inequalities exist in the basic makeup of the church and in theological writing concerning women, doubt may be cast on the whole validity of the religious experience. Women are not interested in being second-class citizens, either in an earthly organization or a heavenly city which ignores their claims to personhood, equality, and even identity. Therefore, the question must be raised as to whether this is really Christ's intention as revealed in the New Testament.

In all four Gospels, Jesus is never reported as acting or speaking to women in a derogatory fashion. He always treated them as equals, individuals, and persons. He testified in his practice and in his doctrine that he saw woman, as created by God, equal to man, endorsing the view of Genesis 1:27: "So God created man in his own image, in the image of God he created him; male and female he created them."

When you realize that Jesus spoke to women in a society where they were often treated more like chattels than persons, where they usually had no say about who their marriage partners would be, or whether they would be married at all, where they had no opportunity for education or employment equal to a man's, his outlook becomes all the more astounding.

The Israel of the first century was a patriarchal society. The husband was master of his wife. He could divorce her but she could not divorce him. As a daughter a female could be sold into slavery. A woman's husband was chosen for her by her father; it was not necessary for a girl to consent to the choice. In Hebrew rites women were seen as "unclean" and were segregated to a certain section of the temple during the service. Every Hebrew man recited a prayer to thank God that he had not been born a slave, a pagan, or a woman. In the time when Christ lived it was a subject of rabbinical discussion as to whether women had souls at all. There were rabbinical injunctions not to speak to women on the street at all—not even members of the rabbi's own family! Surely the statement of Jesus in John 16:33 would be most appropriate for the women of his day in Palestine: "In the world you have tribulation; but be of good cheer, I have overcome the world."

Some of the reactions of Jesus were, of course, dependent on his human condition as a first-century Jew. But his reaction to the essential person-ness of women transcended his training and pierces through time and history. He treated everyone he encountered as a *person:* the rich young ruler and the beggar at the gates, the Roman centurion and the fishermen, the tax collector and the leper, the blind man and the visionary, the elders and children, the Pharisees and the ignorant, the sinners and temple priests, men and women.

Shirley Chisholm has said that "America, as a nation, is both racist and antifeminist." So was Palestine in the time of Jesus. Yet, he told the parable of the good Samaritan and, worse yet, revealed to the *woman* of Samaria that he was the long-awaited Messiah. He was not blocked in his relationship to people by the traditions and prejudices of his era.

In an attempt to pinpoint his relationship to women more clearly, this book proposes to examine his encounters with women in the New Testament. One thing emerges very clearly: he touched the life of every type of woman—young and old, pious and impious, the religious woman and the sinner, mother and daughter, women who were sick physically and mentally, women who were active, women who were contemplative, women who were concerned about themselves, and women who were concerned for others. These women do not exist only in history; they are prototypes of every kind of woman today. We propose to examine the biblical stories, not only in their historical context but as they apply to the outlooks and concerns of contemporary woman.

In this task our main emphasis is on the reality revealed in the encounter, both for the woman and for Jesus. We are not interested in presenting a picture of pious sentimentality but rather in reconstructing a model appropriate to today's issues. One must bear in mind that many writers of biblical commentary are men. They have often managed to get through whole books on the life of Jesus with no mention of women at all except for an obligatory reference to his mother. Those who have included the role of women in their commentary have often seemed to be on the outside looking in rather than getting to the heart of the matter. However, as in *The Interpreter's Bible*, there are some notable exceptions to this. Some books on women in the Bible have tended to put women in a special category—like *Flowers Mentioned in the Bible and Their Meaning*—rather than see them as persons active in responding to Jesus. We hope that this examination of the encounters of women with Jesus will be helpful in seeing his extraordinary relevance to the personhood of women today.

1

Women Heroines of the Old Testament

While the main emphasis of this book is on the relationship of women to Jesus as shown in the New Testament, it is instructive to evaluate briefly the view of women in the Old Testament to serve as a background and contrast to New Testament encounters.

Although many women appear in the pages of the Old Testament, most are shown in their relationship to men—Sarah, the wife of Abraham, Isaac and Rebecca, Jacob with Leah and Rachel, etc. Four women stand out as heroines in their own right: Deborah, Jael, Judith, and Esther. These women have very vivid personalities and have been favorite subjects for much Christian art. Their stories are fascinating, written in times of tumult, war, and catastrophe.

Deborah, who lived in the time of the Judges of Israel, around 1194–54 B.C., had been elected to a position of great responsibility in the nation.

Now Deborah, a prophetess, the wife of Lappidoth, was judging Israel at that time. She used to sit under the palm of Deborah between Ramah and Bethel in the hill country of Ephraim; and the people of Israel came up to her for judgment.—Judges 4:4–5

So begins the story of Deborah, who called Barak to be her general against the nine hundred iron chariots of Sisera, general of the Canaanites under King Jabin.

15

Deborah must have been a woman of great presence and courage, because Barak refused to lead the army unless she would go with them.

Barak said to her, "If you will go with me, I will go; but if you will not go with me, I will not go." And she said, "I will surely go with you; nevertheless, the road on which you are going will not lead to your glory, for the Lord will sell Sisera into the hand of a woman."—Judges 4:8–9

The Israelites were afraid of the latest military equipment: the iron chariots of the Canaanites. In spite of their technology, the Canaanites were routed by a sudden storm and the overflowing of the river Kishon, which transformed the plain into a sea of mud; all the chariots were stuck and rendered useless for battle.

And Barak pursued the chariots and the army to Harosheth-ha-goiim, and all the army of Sisera fell by the edge of the sword; not a man was left.—Judges 4:16

Meanwhile, a second heroine enters the story: Jael, the wife of Heber the Kenite. She offered the fleeing General Sisera hospitality in her tent, gave him milk, and covered him when he, worn out by flight, lay down to rest.

But Jael the wife of Heber took a tent peg, and took a hammer in her hand, and went softly to him and drove the peg into his temple, till it went down into the ground, as he was lying fast asleep from weariness. So he died.—Judges 4:21

When Barak came by pursuing Sisera, Jael showed him her victim. In the wake of the victory over the Canaanites, Israel had forty years of peace.

A heroine similar to Jael is introduced in the book of Judith, found in the Old Testament Apocrypha. In this story a beautiful widow named Judith, of the town of Bethulia, saves her people when Holofernes, Nebuchadnezzar's general, besieges the town and cuts off the water supply.

Judith, whose name means "the Jewess," dresses in her best array.

> She removed the sackcloth she was wearing and, taking off her widow's dress, she washed all over, anointed herself with costly perfumes, dressed her hair, wrapped a turban round it and put on the dress she used to wear on joyful occasions when her husband Manasseh was alive. She put sandals on her feet, put on her necklaces, bracelets, rings, earrings and all her jewellery, and made herself beautiful enough to catch the eye of every man who saw her.—Judith 10:3–4, JB

She leaves Bethulia and when the Assyrians intercept her and ask where she is going, she replies:

> I am a daughter of the Hebrews . . . and I am fleeing from them since they will soon be your prey. I am on my way to see Holofernes, the general of your army, to give him trustworthy information. I will show him the road to take if he wants to capture all the highlands without losing one man or one life.—Judith 10:12–13, JB

Judith and her maid are shown in to Holofernes, all men marveling at her beauty. She falls on her face before him, begging, "Please listen favourably to what your slave has to say." Holofernes admires her greatly and invites her to a banquet, hoping to seduce her. When the other guests leave, he collapses on his bed, drunk, and Judith cuts off his head with his own sword. She returns to Bethulia and shows the head of Holofernes to her people, advising them to attack the leaderless army which was fleeing in panic. The story ends with the Israelites looting the Assyrian camp and giving Holofernes' furniture to Judith. Although Judith attracted many suitors, she remained a widow and lived to the ripe age of one hundred five, surrounded by possessions.

It is fairly obvious from this account that Judith was exceptionally beautiful, independent, and intelligent. It is equally obvious that she was not above being used as a sex object in a righteous cause and was devious, deceitful, and servile in her dealings. She placed the welfare of her people first and would be unscrupulous in order to gain victory for her nation.

A final heroine from the Old Testament is Esther, the queen who saved her people. A consensus of authorities seems to be that this story is probably a blend of fact and fiction, much like a historical novel. Xerxes (or Ahasuerus), the king mentioned in the story, was the son of Darius and actually ruled Persia from 486 to 465 B.C.

The story of Esther from the book of Esther, goes as follows: King Xerxes, feeling high from the wine at a banquet, called his queen, Vashti, so he could show off her beauty to the guests. She refused to come, so he decided to depose her as an example to all Persian women who might decide to defy their lords and masters as a result.

To find a successor to Queen Vashti, all the beautiful young virgins of Persia were brought to the palace, among them Esther, a Jewish orphan who had been adopted by her cousin Mordecai. She was told by Mordecai not to speak of her people and her descent. Esther pleased the king above all the others, and she became queen in place of Vashti.

Haman, the prime minister, conceived a hatred for Mordecai because Mordecai, as a good Jew, would not bow down and worship him. To be revenged on Mordecai, Haman persuaded the king to sign a decree to exterminate all the Jews in his kingdom. In these dire straits Mordecai appealed to his cousin, the queen, to save her people by interceding for them with the king.

Esther replied, "All the king's courtiers are well aware that death is the penalty for any man or woman who approaches the king in his court without being summoned, unless the king extends his golden sceptre, and I have not been summoned to come to the King for the past thirty days!" (See Esther 4:11.)

However, she agreed to go to the king if the Jews would fast for three days for her success, "And if I perish, I perish!"

On the third day, Esther took her life in her hands and approached the king in his inner court. He extended the golden scepter to her and she won his favor. After a series of maneuvers, she had Haman hanged on the scaffold he had prepared for Mordecai and saved her people from destruction.

Esther stood to lose her status as queen, her luxurious existence in the palace, even her life if the king did not admit her to his presence. She risked everything for her people, knowing this bond was the strongest she could have.

All she had to counter the power of the politician Haman was her beauty and the king's regard. Her husband, a typical Oriental despot, had the power of life and death over his subjects in his absolute control. As his treatment of his former queen, Vashti, shows, he could be capricious and revoke all the glory of his queen in a moment. It was, therefore, in great fear and with great cunning that Esther succeeded in her plan to defeat Haman and rescue her people from the decree of death.

Some striking facts emerge from these four stories. First, all these women brought deliverance to their people in time of trouble. They were regarded as heroines by the Jews—women who by their own power had diverted catastrophe from the Israelite nation. They were national figures—women who had acted for the Hebrew people in a time of great need.

They were all exceptional characters. Deborah and Jael had great courage and were able to take on belligerent, almost masculine roles when faced with an enemy. Judith and Esther, on the other hand, were women of unusual beauty, who used all their feminine wiles to accomplish their task. They were clever and ruthless and well aware of their sexual attractiveness as an asset. However, all these women did not act for themselves or by their own impulse; they worked for a cause greater than themselves and with the urging of their communities or allegiances.

These Old Testament heroines were honored as individuals because of their special abilities and the accomplishment of specific tasks rather than recognized as persons in their own right. They were celebrated because they deserved praise for their actions, not because they could lay any claim to individuality or personhood by their creation as human beings. They were unusual rather than average women, talented beyond common expectations. History had marked them for a special place and a special respect that they could not expect as women. Their claim to personhood was one of achievement and not of humanity. They were specially favored of

God, an instrument of his policy. They were the exception rather than the rule for womankind in Israel.

It is difficult to identify with these women of the Old Testament in their chauvinistic policy of Israel first by any means. The circumstances and surroundings of their world seem foreign to us, either as a war leader or the wife of an Oriental potentate. Deborah, Jael, Judith, and Esther, dramatic as their stories are, remain somewhat distant from us, embedded firmly in the matrix of Israel's heroic history.

2

Mary, the Mother of Jesus

In the sixth month the angel Gabriel was sent from God to a city of Galilee named Nazareth, to a virgin betrothed to a man whose name was Joseph, of the house of David; and the virgin's name was Mary. And he came to her and said, "Hail, O favored one, the Lord is with you!" But she was greatly troubled at the saying, and considered in her mind what sort of greeting this might be. And the angel said to her, "Do not be afraid, Mary, for you have found favor with God. And behold, you will conceive in your womb and bear a son, and you shall call his name Jesus. . . . And Mary said, "Behold, I am the handmaid of the Lord; let it be to me according to your word." And the angel departed from her.—Luke 1:26–31, 38

Mary has been made into a model for all women, particularly in the Roman Catholic Church, so it is very important to see what her true character was like and to pierce the veils of sentimentality that surround her. The apotheosis of Mary has tended to obscure her human qualities as a woman and a person.

There is no question that she was at this time a devout young woman, able to receive the word of God. And yet, she does not receive it blindly but looks intelligently at its implications. She accepts God's mission for her after fully understanding it. She is obedient to the will of God.

Much has been made of this obedience. Mary has been used as an example of obedience, especially feminine obedience, because of her

21

reply, "Behold, I am the handmaid of the Lord." This docility has been lauded as an appropriate *feminine* virtue, especially by masculine writers. The Bible does not have it that way. Obedience to the will of God is a virtue for both men and women. In Matthew 1:18–21, Joseph is enjoined by a dream to be obedient to God's will and take Mary as his wife. Joseph also obeys the messenger of God when he is told to take Mary and Jesus into Egypt to escape Herod's slaughter (Matthew 2:13–15).

In the Old Testament there are innumerable examples of the obedience of men to God's will, from Abraham on down. In fact, in terms of quantitative analysis, obedience would seem to be more appropriate to men, as more men in the Bible were instructed in it than women!

However, it is quite clear that obedience to God's will is a desirable human trait, not belonging either to men or women exclusively. We twist the scripture out of context if we assign obedience to one sex only.

In the long run, the use of obedience as a feminine virtue only distorts the quality of family life and starts a subtle discrimination against women. If women are to be obedient, who is to give them orders? Men, of course. And so girls are raised to be more responsive and obedient to the demands of others, while boys learn to expect special privileges and to have their own way in many circumstances.

This is a misinterpretation of obedience. The Bible speaks of obedience to God's will, not man's, and applies it across the board, regardless of sex.

Why did God choose Mary to be the mother of Jesus? Mary's situation in life was not exceptional. She was betrothed to a carpenter and was a woman of the working class. She was certainly not the beautifully robed aristocrat who appears in many art masterpieces. Perhaps this was one of the reasons for the choice: Mary was an ordinary woman as all of us are ordinary women and men. As Dorothy Sayers puts it in the play "The Man Born to Be King," "When the Angel's message came to me, the Lord put a song in my heart. I suddenly saw that wealth and cleverness were nothing to God—no one is too unimportant to be His friend." [1]

Mary was pure, devout, and responsive but she was not super-woman. God's gift of his son to the world came through an ordinary woman, an untitled member of humanity, a partaker in God's own creation. She did not think of herself as special. She accepted her task with joy. What a difficult undertaking it turned out to be.

And Joseph also went up from Galilee, from the city of Nazareth, to Judea, to the city of David, which is called Bethlehem, because he was of the house and lineage of David, to be enrolled with Mary, his betrothed, who was with child. And while they were there, the time came for her to be delivered. And she gave birth to her first-born son and wrapped him in swaddling cloths, and laid him in a manger, because there was no place for them in the inn.—Luke 2:4–7

The story of Christ's birth is often so shrouded in sentimentality that we do not see it for what it truly was. As T. S. Eliot has one of the wise men say in his poem "Journey of the Magi":

> I had seen birth and death,
> But had thought they were different; this Birth was
> Hard and bitter agony for us . . .[2]

Almost at term, Mary had to travel the hard journey from Nazareth to Bethlehem. She could not have wanted to go but was forced to make the trip at the command of the Roman rulers of her country. She was away from her home and her kinfolk who should have been with her at the birth of her first child. There was no room to stay at the inn, where at least there would have been comfort and women to help her through childbirth. Her child was born in a shelter for animals, laid in a manger because there was no cradle ready. Jesus was born almost as an outcast in society. His mother faced conditions as difficult as any mother has endured. Despite the gifts that were to come, it was scarcely a pampered birth. In this hard initiation into motherhood, Mary shared the lot of the most underprivileged of mothers.

When they saw the star, they rejoiced exceedingly with great joy; and going into the house they saw the child with Mary his mother,

and they fell down and worshiped him. Then, opening their treasures, they offered him gifts, gold and frankincense and myrrh.—Matthew 2:10–11

The wise men brought gifts of gold, frankincense, and myrrh—the best gifts men could offer. It has been commented that gold stood for the things of this world and possibly kingship, frankincense was an incense symbolizing worship, while myrrh, a burial spice, stood for death.

These were appropriate gifts from the Eastern sages to one who was to be king of the Jews, as they interpreted the appearance of the star. Mary must have been surprised, perhaps overwhelmed, when these gifts were offered to her infant son. She might have been filled with pride as a simple peasant woman receiving gifts fit for a king. It would have been easy to overvalue their importance.

Yet, some quality of her motherhood must have held restraint and a true evaluation of the worth of the gifts of this world, because her son ultimately rejected all these offerings and all the temptations involved in accepting them. There may possibly be a parallel between the three gifts of the wise men and the three temptations of Jesus in the wilderness as reported in Matthew 4:1–11 and Luke 4:1–13. The parallel to the Lucan version seems even closer than to that in Matthew. The first temptation was to turn stones into bread, an important factual necessity of life, much like the first gift of gold, the currency of this life. The second temptation was to be given the kingdoms of the world if Jesus would worship the devil, paralleling the gift of frankincense, a representation of worship. The final temptation was to throw himself from the pinnacle of the temple, to flirt with death, analogous to the gift of myrrh, a symbol of death.

Jesus did not do any of the things expected of him. He did not seek the power of wealth or kingship. He did not yield to the insidious pressure to become an object of adulation and worship among his followers. Instead he gave an example of servanthood in his washing of his disciples' feet. Finally, he did not succumb to death, the usual conclusion of this life, but fought free of the grave in God's plan for him in the resurrection. None of the expectations of this world were relevant for Jesus. He followed God's plan instead. And this openness to the will of God was surely in part a heritage from his mother, Mary.

Mary is seen most significantly as a mother—a mother who influenced and formed the early life of Jesus. Did she raise a passive, dependent child? Or was Jesus able to go beyond the confines of his home and even on occasion reject the claims of his mother?

Two episodes stand out very clearly. The first occurred when Jesus was twelve years old and went with his family to Jerusalem. When the feast of Passover was over, his family returned to Nazareth but discovered on the route home that Jesus was missing. They searched for him among the company of pilgrims without success, then returned to Jerusalem. After three days Mary and Joseph found Jesus in the temple, listening and asking questions of the teachers there. His mother said, "Son, why have you treated us this way? Your father and I have been looking for you everywhere."

Jesus didn't fold with contrition. Instead he showed his awareness of other ties beyond his home in his reply, "Didn't you know I must be about my Father's business?" He returned home and was obedient to his family, but it is obvious that he was not dependent on them. His mother had allowed him the freedom to become himself and to become aware of his mission.

Later, when he had begun his formal ministry, he asserted his independence even more strongly and ultimately proclaimed his freedom from home ties.

While he was still speaking to the people, behold, his mother and his brothers stood outside, asking to speak to him. But he replied to the man who told him, "Who is my mother, and who are my brothers?" And stretching out his hand toward his disciples, he said, "Here are my mother and my brothers! For whoever does the will of my Father in heaven is my brother, and sister, and mother."—Matthew 12:46–50

What a contemporary ring this answer has! It is scarcely the reply of a man who has been smothered by his mother. But before we start speculating on the generation gap, we should be aware that the purpose of the reply was not to put down his mother but to point to the ultimate allegiance of Christian life.

Still, this episode does demonstrate that Mary's motherhood was a difficult one. She had to give up claims on her son which he could not fulfill because his own mission occupied him to the exclusion of other ties.

The testimony to Mary's motherhood can be seen in the qualities which she gave to her son. These qualities were present in her life and appear again and again in the record of the ministry of Jesus. First of all, there was courage—the courage that led her to accept the will of God for her, the courage that brought her to the foot of the cross. This courage Jesus showed all through his life. In preaching his revolutionary doctrine he did not underestimate the power of opposition, but he had the courage to persist.

Mary also had great faith in God. She committed her life to God's hands, as did her son. She was faithful to the commands of God and she was faithful in her relationship to her son. Jesus knew the power of this quality in everyday life, and time and time again said to those he healed, "Your faith has made you whole."

Humility is not a virtue that has been played up much of late, but it is a rare and wonderful gift in life. Many people are very self-important; they never have the humility to recognize their limitations or to acknowledge a power outside themselves. Mary had the rare quality of humility which allowed her to accept the wonder of a power greater than herself. Jesus, with all his fantastic gifts and abilities, had this same humility. He never exalted himself; he always pointed to God in his works.

Jesus also learned obedience from Mary. Both were obedient to the will of God. And both were, as Isaiah 53:3 puts it, "acquainted with grief." They knew the cost of living on this earth. Mary gave to Jesus the quality of endurance—the endurance which persists despite obstacles, despite misunderstandings, despite threats.

And Mary must have taught Jesus from an early age respect for women as persons. He knew her as a full human being, and he treated all the women he met as individuals, following this example.

Certainly Mary showed her loving spirit in her relationship with her son, and he carried this human love into all his contacts with people. His open relationship to children and the tenderness with which he treated them were reflections of his own childhood. They were all children of God, but they were children of women also—women like his mother, Mary.

Mary has another special distinction in the Gospels. According to the Gospel of John, she was the instigator of Christ's first miracle.

On the third day there was a marriage at Cana in Galilee, and the mother of Jesus was there; Jesus also was invited to the marriage, with his disciples. When the wine failed, the mother of Jesus said to him, "They have no wine." And Jesus said to her, "O woman, what have you to do with me? My hour is not yet come." His mother said to the servants, "Do whatever he tells you."—John 2:1–5

The story goes on to tell how the servants filled large jars with water. When the jars were brought to the marriage feast, the water was changed into the best wine.

This story reveals several interesting points. First, it shows how Mary understood both the situation and Jesus. She knew he would not fail her in a crisis, even though he protested that his time had not yet come. It is really a marvelous, almost humorous picture of the mother taking the whole situation in and then telling the servants to obey her son. The give and take of the relationship of mother and son stands forth incandescently.

Then, the story is an interesting commentary on the fact that the first miracle that Jesus performed was at the request of a woman—almost provoked by a woman. It reflects on a special quality of the relationship of Jesus to women. He never ignored them. He understood their needs and responded to their concerns. He neither dismissed women as unimportant drudges nor did he pay them lip service only, with elaborate compliments to their superiority but no recognition of their problems or legitimate demands.

Another facet of this story, remarked on by many scholars, is the indication that sections of the Gospel of John were probably inspired by Mary herself. The story of the marriage at Cana, as well as the narrative of Mary at the foot of the cross receiving the words of

Christ, and several other episodes involving Mary are found only in the fourth Gospel. This has led to speculation that Mary told these experiences to the writer of the fourth Gospel, who incorporated the material in his account along with other sources.

Mary could not have understood fully Christ's ministry on earth, but she must have worried when he denounced the Pharisees and rulers of the synagogue. She may have feared that the hostility of the temple hierarchy would threaten her son's life. She saw Jesus drawing away from the normal expectations of Jewish life, and this must have been disturbing to her. She perceived that Jesus was becoming a hero to many people but probably realized this very heroism made him a threat to the rulers of Israel, who wished to keep peace with Rome.

What Mary feared or possibly foresaw came to pass in the capture, trial, and crucifixion of Jesus. Mary was a witness to the death of her son.

But standing by the cross of Jesus were his mother, and his mother's sister, Mary the wife of Clopas, and Mary Magdalene. When Jesus saw his mother, and the disciple whom he loved standing near, he said to his mother, "Woman, behold your son!" Then he said to the disciple, "Behold your mother!" And from that hour the disciple took her to his own home.—John 19:25-27

While Jesus was dying in agony upon the cross, he still remembered his mother and made provision for her. He did not give her empty words of consolation or call to her for help. He acknowledged fully the tie of sonship and gave her another son to take care of her. He did not give her a son in name only, but one who would truly assume the duties and loving relationship of a son. In the hour of death he remembered the claim of Mary, perhaps even responded to her desolation and loss. In the bitterest hour of her life Mary received her highest tribute.

Love calls forth love, and Jesus had learned from Mary that love is not just an abstract word: it is the sharing of joys and sorrows. Jesus knew that love has responsibilities, and he acknowledged these responsibilities in his words from the cross. These words, more than anything else, testify to the strength of Mary's love for her son and of his for her.

The role that Mary has played in Christian doctrine has obscured our view of her as a real human being. The Christian church has often put her on a pedestal and has not understood her profound qualities as a person. Theologically, particularly in the Roman Catholic Church, Mary has been referred to as the New Eve, as Christ is the New Adam. Mary is seen as revoking the curse of Genesis when the first man and woman were exiled from the Garden of Eden for eating of the forbidden tree of the knowledge of good and evil. However, the liberating factors of Mary's role have not been fully explored. If the curse of Genesis is revoked by Mary's acceptance of God's will, then it follows that the old injunction of women being subordinate to their husbands is also revoked. The whole Hebrew structure of women being "unclean" and unfit for certain occupations, based on Eve's subordination, also falls. Mary is the originator of a new order, a new Christian understanding of women. This new understanding liberates women from the concepts of their secondary role in the Old Testament and frees them to express their full humanity.

Mary's theological significance is extremely important to the role of women today, but so is her life as a woman. Her example of creative motherhood and courageous endurance in the face of disaster is an inspiration and an encouragement to every woman. There is no need to sentimentalize the character of Mary: the reality of her life is much more compelling. There is no need to put her on a pedestal: her qualities are a passport to high esteem. We do her an injustice if we see only her sainthood and not her womanhood.

> My soul magnifies the Lord,
> and my spirit rejoices in God my Savior,
> for he has regarded the low estate of his handmaiden.
> For behold, henceforth all generations will call me blessed;
> for he who is mighty has done great things for me,
> and holy is his name.—Luke 1:46–49

3

Elizabeth, the Barren Woman

In the days of Herod, king of Judea, there was a priest named Zechariah, of the division of Abijah; and he had a wife . . . and her name was Elizabeth. And they were both righteous before God, walking in all the commandments and ordinances of the Lord blameless. But they had no child, because Elizabeth was barren, and both were advanced in years.

Now while he was serving as priest before God when his division was on duty, according to the custom of the priesthood, it fell to him by lot to enter the temple of the Lord and burn incense. And the whole multitude of the people were praying outside at the hour of incense. And there appeared to him an angel of the Lord standing on the right side of the altar of incense. And Zechariah was troubled when he saw him, and fear fell upon him. But the angel said to him, "Do not be afraid, Zechariah, for your prayer is heard, and your wife Elizabeth will bear you a son, and you shall call his name John. . . .

After these days his wife Elizabeth conceived, and for five months she hid herself, saying, "Thus the Lord has done to me in the days when he looked on me, to take away my reproach among men.— Luke 1:5–13, 24–25

For many years Elizabeth was childless. Not only did she yearn for children, but being barren was looked upon as a social stigma in Israel. Childlessness was seen as a reproach among the Hebrews and sterility was considered the woman's fault in Old Testament accounts. A good example of this attitude is seen in Genesis 30:1–2 when Rachel, after her sister Leah had borne four sons and she herself was still childless, said to her husband Jacob, "Give me children, or I shall die!" Jacob, angered, replied, "Am I in God's place? It is he that has refused you children."

Motherhood is often seen in the Bible as the gift of God. There are prototypes of the account of Elizabeth's having a son in the stories of Abraham and Sarah, who were also advanced in years (Genesis 17:16–19), and of Manoah and his wife (Judges 13:2–24), parents of Samson. In all these cases there is a special mission marked out for the child, one which is accepted by his parents.

Elizabeth was the cousin of Mary, the mother of Jesus. After the annunciation to Mary, when Elizabeth was six months pregnant, she went to visit her cousin.

In those days Mary arose and went with haste into the hill country, to a city of Judah, and she entered the house of Zechariah and greeted Elizabeth. And when Elizabeth heard the greeting of Mary, the babe leaped in her womb; and Elizabeth was filled with the Holy Spirit and she exclaimed with a loud cry, "Blessed are you among women, and blessed is the fruit of your womb."—Luke 1:39–42

It has been speculated that Mary visited Elizabeth when she found she was to bear a child because Mary's mother was probably dead, and Elizabeth may have been Mary's closest living relative. It seems a testimony to Elizabeth's character that Mary should seek her out. In spite of Elizabeth's long childlessness, she was obviously motherly in her feelings toward Mary, which is one reason why Mary went to her cousin's house to stay. Elizabeth must have been warm and receptive to her and treated her as a daughter. Such women often have many children of the spirit. As Isaiah 54:1 puts it:

> Sing, O barren one, who did not bear;
> > break forth into singing and cry aloud,
> > you who have not been in travail!

> For the children of the desolate
>> one will be more
>>> than the children of her that is
>>>> married, says the Lord.

Motherliness is not only characteristic of those who have had their own children. Sometimes this quality is found more in unmarried women, such as the teacher who encourages her students and truly develops them through her caring. Bertolt Brecht expressed this thought in the last act of "The Caucasian Chalk Circle." The judge awards custody of the young prince to the nurse who took care of him in a time of flight, rather than to his mother who deserted him, saying that mothering is not just giving birth to a child, but that a person becomes a mother by mothering, by really caring for a child, and sacrificing for him. So Elizabeth, formerly barren, was a true mother to Mary in a time of crisis. She herself found new life and recognized life in others.

Now the time came for Elizabeth to be delivered, and she gave birth to a son. And her neighbors and kinsfolk heard that the Lord had shown great mercy to her, and they rejoiced with her. And on the eighth day they came to circumcise the child; and they would have named him Zechariah after his father, but his mother said, "Not so; he shall be called John." And they said to her, "None of your kindred is called by this name." And they made signs to his father, inquiring what he would have him called. And he asked for a writing tablet, and wrote, "His name is John." And they all marveled. And immediately his mouth was opened and his tongue loosed, and he spoke, blessing God.—Luke 1:57–64

Both Elizabeth and Zechariah accepted God's message and insisted on an unfamiliar, nonfamily name for their son. Although it was customary to name a son after his father, Elizabeth and Zechariah did not follow the tradition, because another name had been given to the child by God.

In a broader sense this might indicate that the parents did not insist on their son growing up in the family stereotype. His name would not be a straitjacket of family customs and expectations. They were willing to let him develop on his own and become a person in his own right. Perhaps Elizabeth and Zechariah realized that families do not own their children; they only nurture them. They had reason to see John as a special gift from God, but the same holds true for all parents and children. How many women are as wise as Elizabeth in letting their children develop on their own, find their own identity?

Several things can be surmised about the character of Elizabeth. She was responsive to the word of God, capable of understanding his power in her life and in the lives of others. Elizabeth was perceptive: she immediately realized that Mary would be the mother of the savior of Israel. Many other women in her circumstance would have been so taken up with their own pregnancy that they never would have recognized the radiant expectation of Mary. But Elizabeth was not one of these. She reached out to Mary, she acknowledged her, and she sheltered her as a mother would.

Occasionally in church art Elizabeth is symbolized by a great rock. This may stand for her long barrenness, but it can also be interpreted as a sign of security and protection. Elizabeth was like the Rock of Gibraltar: stable, steady, and unmoved. She was "solid as a rock" in her relationship to her cousin, offering her welcome and protection.

Elizabeth was unselfish in her recognition of Mary's role. She rejoiced with her in the coming of Jesus. There may not be many Elizabeths in this world, but when we meet them we are glad. They are the generous spirits who can see beyond their own concerns and share in the joys of others. They are the ones who are steady fortresses of comfort in times of crisis. They are those who bring new life into the world at a time when the world least expects it.

It seems strange that after all the centuries of so-called civilization, not being able to have children is still often a social stigma, as if a woman is not fully a woman unless she has had children. We don't evaluate men in this way. Yet, unless medical evidence is produced to the contrary, the wife is held responsible for sterility and many times feels guilty about it. In some childless women the sense of social isolation is extreme; some actually develop neurotic reactions about their state, whether they adopt children or not.

It is as unfair to judge women by their child-producing capacities as it would be to judge men by the same criterion. If we lived in a semi-tribal society, as the early Hebrews did, and more children would mean a stronger tribe, there might be some justification for regarding multiple childbirth as a laudatory accomplishment; but we do not. We live in a highly sophisticated technological society where the resources of the world are being strained to keep up with population growth. Under these circumstances, contemporary ideas of controlled family planning, zero population growth, or adopting children already born are much wiser. And rather than praising a biological skill in women to the exclusion of other skills, it would make more sense to accept and develop the whole person rather than one segment of that person.

4

The Prophetess Anna

And there was a prophetess, Anna, the daughter of Phanuel, of the tribe of Asher; she was of a great age, having lived with her husband seven years from her virginity, and as a widow till she was eighty-four. She did not depart from the temple, worshiping with fasting and prayer night and day. And coming up at that very hour she gave thanks to God, and spoke of him [Jesus] to all who were looking for the redemption of Jerusalem.—Luke 2:36–38

Here we have before us the brief story of an old woman, a prophetess, who recognized Jesus as the Messiah.

We are told that Anna's father, Phanuel, came from the tribe of Asher, which was well known for its beautiful women. These women often married kings or priests. Anna was married for seven years. When her husband died, she did not remarry but lived as a constant worshiper in the temple where her husband may have served as a priest. Anna was probably childless or she would not have been able to live in the temple but would have stayed home to take care of her child or children. It may not be too much to say that in recognizing the baby Jesus as Israel's Messiah she claimed him as a child of the spirit.

The occasion for her meeting Mary and Joseph with the baby Jesus was the rite of the purification of the mother after the birth of a child. Mary offered a pair of turtle doves in the court of women as a thank-offering for her first-born son. This was followed by the presentation in the temple. The purification ceremony reflected the Hebrew idea of the "uncleanness" of women, while the presentation in the temple was to show the physical perfection of the baby, as rabbinical law held that a child with a defect could not serve in the priesthood.

Anna's recognition of the baby as the Messiah justified her title as a prophetess. In her long preparation in the temple she may have become familiar with Old Testament prophecies relating to a coming Messiah and knew by instinct that the moment had come. Prophecy, as used in the Bible, is not only future prediction but also refers a statement of religious truth in a given situation. In the Old Testament we think of women prophets such as Miriam and Deborah. Anna is the only prophetess mentioned by name in the New Testament, and in a way she really belongs to the Old Testament as a prefigurer of Christ. She is rather like a latter-day Moses who never reached the promised land of Christ's ministry in its fullness. Yet, she could recognize decisively its beginning and witness to it.

Anna was the first woman to publicly acclaim Jesus as the Messiah. In this sense she was really the first woman to be a Christian missionary. She spoke of him to all who were looking for the redemption of Jerusalem. This was not just a private rejoicing, a personal recognition kept personal. Anna shared her insight with everyone. She knew it was good news indeed even if she did not know what form this mission would take. As a result of living in the temple during her widowhood, Anna had avoided the temptations and concerns of everyday life in the city around her, but she had never lost touch with this world. She knew that the message of the Messiah was not a private treasure, and she communicated it to all she could.

Anna's recognition of Jesus as Messiah is paired with Simeon's prophecy about Christ in Luke 2:25–35, which contains the famous lines:

> Lord, now lettest thou thy servant
> depart in peace,
> according to thy word;

for mine eyes have seen thy salvation
which thou hast prepared in the
          presence of all peoples,
a light for revelation to the Gentiles,
and for glory to thy people Israel.

This pairing of a male and female recognition scene is extremely interesting. It implies that Christ came not just to men (or the salvation of humanity understood) but specifically to men and women. The insight that led Simeon to discern Jesus as Messiah was also possessed by Anna. There seems to be an effort in the Gospel to say that men and women are equally important to the kingdom of Jesus and are equally perceptive of him as Messiah.

In a similar way, the Gospels often pair parables about men and about women. Luke, for example, tells of the women and the lost coin that is found (Luke 15:8–10) and about the importunate widow (Luke 18:1–5), while Matthew writes of the woman with leaven being like the kingdom of heaven (Matthew 13:33) and about the wise and foolish virgins (Matthew 25:1–12); Mark gives the story of the widow's mite (Mark 12:41–44). It is evident that Jesus was concerned about reaching his women listeners as well as his men followers and made his point by teachings that were especially meaningful to them. His recognition and his ministry were certainly not "For Men Only" affairs, and this aspect was heralded by Anna's prophecy.

Anna was an old woman with all the grace, experience, intuition, and knowledge of age. In her we can see some valuable characteristics of age, often so little regarded or esteemed.

Anna had great patience. She knew how to wait for important things. She probably studied the prophecies of the past in Isaiah and Micah concerning the promised one that was to come. She believed that there were things worth waiting for and that instant gratification and rewards were not always possible or even desirable.

Her patience was not a passive thing. With it she had persistence. She stayed in the temple where she could study the scriptures and wait for the time to come. She persisted in her dream and was amply rewarded.

Like many older people, she also had enough detachment from the passing scene to recognize revelation when it came. She could evaluate what was important and what was less important. She was not so caught up with the hustle and bustle of activities that she could not see that this ordinary-looking child was really someone quite different. Her detachment made her more sensitive to the significant in life.

She had lived a long life and during this time had gathered many experiences and much knowledge. Hers was the richness of age so little appreciated today.

We live in a culture which promotes youth and does not profit from the wisdom of the old. This is particularly hard on women, as they are supposed to be young and beautiful objects for possession, and the very thought of age becomes an anathema to them and to the culture in general. Anna grew old gracefully and graciously, gaining knowledge and insight with age. These are goals neglected or rejected in our culture today. Age is regarded as obsolescence in a consumer world.

The New Testament does not see it that way. No one is disqualified by age. Growing old is regarded as a way to wisdom and is honored. It has been said that the Christian church today has no place for old people and often does not recognize their needs. This is not true of the pastors who visit the elderly in hospitals, nursing homes, and their own homes, but of the members of the church and their programs. If this is the case, the church must regain its mission to the old, following the precedent of Anna. And those who are old, as Anna, have a great opportunity to discern the new in church life and welcome it.

One problem of the role of elderly persons in church life is that change is threatening to them. We live in an era when the services and teachings in all denominations of the Christian church have been drastically revised. Many older people are accustomed to the earlier forms of worship and cherish them. When these forms are modified or abolished, older people may feel their whole way of life has been altered. Often the change is so unsettling to them that they refuse to participate in church life at all. This is a tragedy, because the reality under the changing forms of liturgy is constant. At the same time, many elderly persons are open to change and modification, and they rejoice in the new life that is brought by it. These are the mainstay of parish activities, and their advice and participation are eagerly sought. The church can and should be a continuing home for older people as the temple was for Anna. Their wisdom and patience are needed.

Women like Anna may be rejected by the contemporary culture as having outgrown their "usefulness." But the message of the Gospel is just the opposite. Anna, the prophetess, stands on the threshold of the New Testament and is honored by her encounter with Jesus, the promised one. The qualities of age are recognized in this encounter and are liberated in the service of the Lord.

5

The Daughter of Jairus

Then came one of the rulers of the synagogue, Jairus by name; and seeing him, he fell at his feet, and besought him, saying, "My little daughter is at the point of death. Come and lay your hands on her, so that she may be made well, and live." And he went with him. . . . While he was still speaking, there came from the ruler's house some who said, "Your daughter is dead. Why trouble the Teacher any further?" But ignoring what they said, Jesus said to the ruler of the synagogue, "Do not fear, only believe." And he allowed no one to follow him except Peter and James and John the brother of James. When they came to the house of the ruler of the synagogue, he saw a tumult, and people weeping and wailing loudly. And when he had entered, he said to them, "Why do you make a tumult and weep? The child is not dead but sleeping." And they laughed at him. But he put them all outside, and took the child's father and mother and those who were with him, and went in where the child was. Taking her by the hand he said to her, "Talitha cumi"; which means, "Little girl, I say to you, arise." And immediately the girl got up and walked; for she was twelve years old. And immediately they were overcome with amazement. And he strictly charged them that no one should know this, and told them to give her something to eat.—Mark 5:22–24, 35–43

Surely this is one of the most vivid encounters in the Synoptic Gospels. You can almost feel the hot streets of the town, with the crowds pressing around the great healer; you can hear the wailing of the mourners.

One thing stands out very strongly: the common sense approach of Christ in the midst of all the hysterical excitement.

First, he calms the father's fears when people come rushing up with the news of his daughter's death. He says, "Do not fear, only believe." And instead of taking the whole crowd of followers with him, he brings only three—Peter, James, and John. When he comes to the house, he sends all the people outside who were crowding into the stuffy little room. This is the first step in the event of any accident or sickness—to disperse the people who are crowding around the victim. And Jesus minimizes the crisis by telling them that the daughter of Jairus is not dead but sleeping.

When he confronts the girl, he does so directly; he doesn't hesitate or sympathize endlessly. He calls her forth decisively: "Little girl, I say to you, arise."

As a final, very common sense approach to the situation, he tells the parents to give the girl something to eat. This is a real response to adolescent needs, as the mother of any teenage daughter could tell you! And yet, no one else seems to have thought of these things.

This is just one of many encounters where the common sense of Jesus is very evident. He showed this sound judgment throughout his entire ministry. For example, in the feeding of the five thousand, Jesus sized up the situation very accurately. He realized that when food was offered, people would run up and some might be hurt in the crowding. He said, "Make them sit down." In this way everyone could be fed in turn. It is very hard to stampede or riot while sitting down.

In a similar way Jesus had a common sense approach to healing on the sabbath. The Jews forbade any work on the sabbath and described healing as work, but Jesus said, "What man of you, if he has one sheep and it falls into a pit on the sabbath, will not lay hold of it and lift it out? Of how much more value is a man than a sheep! (Matt. 12:11–12)." And about another sabbath prohibition, he said, "The sabbath was made for man, not man for the sabbath (Mark 2:27)."

Jesus took the common sense way of convincing Thomas after the resurrection that he was his Lord. He told Thomas to feel the wounds from the crucifixion. He knew that this material proof would silence the doubts of his follower. Thomas responded, "My Lord and my God! (John 20:28)."

The story of Jairus' daughter could be called the story of an adolescent crisis. The girl was twelve and in Israel of that day girls matured early. They were betrothed and married shortly after physical maturity, which usually comes by age twelve, if not before. The shock of change and growing up, the transition from child to young woman may have been overwhelming for the daughter of Jairus.

Her father sounds as if he were overprotective of her. He said "my little daughter," but she was twelve years old and probably an adolescent already. In Luke 8:42 we are told she was his only daughter. It is likely she was the spoiled and petted child of her father. It must have been very difficult for her to face leaving this secure and coddled childhood for the uncertainties of adolescence and the responsibilities of womanhood.

It is possible that she may have withdrawn from the difficulties of her situation, dropped out psychologically, torn between the conflicting desires to remain a child and the demands to become a woman.

We do not know all the facts of the situation, but Jesus' words seem to suggest the possibility that she was not dead, but possibly in a coma. This could have been a catatonic state, a form of schizophrenia. It is basically a refusal to face up to a terrifying reality and a total retreat from life into a frozen state of immobility either in a catatonic trance or hysterical paralysis.

Jesus called Jairus' daughter back to reality from an actual death or a psychological death. In this encounter he was a real savior to the adolescent who had collapsed before the problems of her situation. He spoke unambiguously, authoritatively, and bridged the way for her from death to life.

The crisis situation of the daughter of Jairus is not unlike the problems of adolescents today. Adolescence is a period of rapid physical and emotional change. Some of these changes of mood create feelings of alienation, aloneness, and a desire for withdrawal from the problems of growing up. Adolescence is a classic time for identity crises. A young person is no longer sure who he or she is. Changes have been too rapid to cope with. A very common psychological disease of adolescence is schizophrenia. A schizophrenic does not know who he is. Sometimes he is in a divided state with several personalities. Sometimes reality becomes so threatening he retreats into a catatonic state or hysterical paralysis.

Even without these extreme personality disorders, adolescence is often painful and difficult. There are problems of communication between parents and children, between the adolescent and his brothers and sisters, and even between the adolescent and his peer group. Noncommunication is often shown in such antisocial behavior as playing music so loudly that people cannot talk over the din. It's sometimes easier to listen to noise than to other people.

For this generation, taking drugs has often been a way of avoiding immediate problems. Questions of identity, future career, and present problems can be held in abeyance in a drug-induced trance. That threatening reality is somewhere else when we are on a "trip."

Drugs can also be dangerous and for some they are a sign of a flirtation with death. Adolescents are often infatuated with death and like to test themselves against danger. For some suicide seems the only way out.

This is a time for "turning off" for some adolescents. In the more extreme cases their behavior approaches that of autistic children, who have been so frightened by reality that they have almost totally rejected it. There was one young woman who, in early adolescence, found life so overwhelming and confusing that she took to her bed for a year. She couldn't get up, she couldn't move around. This used to be called a nervous breakdown. Now it is cited as a personality disorder or a total "turning off." The problem remains the same. The real world is too threatening. An earlier generation said arrogantly, "Stop the world, I want to get off." This generation of young people seems to say it will stop itself since it can't stop the world and it can't relate to it.

Many times girls tend to retreat into more inner behavior. Today the idea of being a woman is often seen ambiguously. The responsibilities of being a woman are frightening to one approaching physical maturity. At one and the same time a woman is supposed to be a sex symbol, an efficient housekeeper, a good mother, a charming hostess, a helpmate, either an intellectual equal or a delightful birdbrain, and yet she also becomes a nonperson, a role, a function but not a total individual. She may have a career *if* it doesn't interfere with her marriage or her family, and *if* she doesn't mind getting less pay for the same job a man is doing and fewer promotion opportunities. It is not surprising that many adolescent and college-age girls hide their femininity in unisex clothes, blue jeans, and workmen's overalls. Who wants to be identified as a member of the second sex? Or even live up to the idea of a continually alluring sex symbol?

Although they are frequently most acute in adolescence, we all share the problems Jairus' daughter may have faced. How many women have not known feelings of inadequacy before the expectations of our culture? Or a lack of confidence in the face of the demands laid upon us? For even the most sanguine, there come periods of depression, a feeling of "I just want to lie down and die." Like the teen-ager in crisis, we long to drop out of a round of activities which all of a sudden seem meaningless or a job that is too demanding or too mechanical. We revolt against the pressures of our circumstances and listlessness sets in. Nothing evokes a response; nothing seems to affect us. Nothing interests us any more. It requires a recognition of our problems and something stronger than ourselves to pull us out of this state.

In this episode with the daughter of Jairus, Jesus manifested more than his power as a healer. He demonstrated his whole approach to human beings. He was direct, not ambiguous. His speech, one of the few in the Bible recorded in the original Aramaic, was exact and compelling. He was authoritative in taking matters of life and death into his hands. He spoke with authority and not as the scribes, who always quoted passages from Old Testament scripture to back up their opinions.

The encounter with Jairus' daughter shows that Jesus did not deny life but embraced it. This is the essence of the doctrine of the incarnation, the Word become flesh, dwelling among us. In this affirmation of life he said to Jairus' daughter, "You can grow. Don't give up. Life holds more for you than the confusions and defeats you now see and feel."

Jesus gave her strength and encouragement to fulfill her potential. He liberated her from her fear of the conflicts of adolescence and the devastation of the death of her spirit.

6

The Sick Woman

And there was a woman who had had a flow of blood for twelve years, and who had suffered much under many physicians, and had spent all that she had, and was no better but rather grew worse. She had heard the reports about Jesus, and came up behind him in the crowd and touched his garment. For she said, "If I touch even his garments, I shall be made well." And immediately the hemorrhage ceased; and she felt in her body that she was healed of her disease. And Jesus, perceiving in himself that power had gone forth from him, immediately turned about in the crowd, and said, "Who touched my garments?" And his disciples said to him, "You see the crowd pressing around you, and yet you say, 'Who touched me?'" And he looked around to see who had done it. But the woman, knowing what had been done to her, came in fear and trembling, and fell down before him, and told him the whole truth. And he said to her, "Daughter, your faith has made you well; go in peace, and be healed of your disease."—Mark 5:25–34

This episode of the sick woman is sandwiched in the middle of the account of Jesus healing Jairus' daughter. It is a story full of the drama and pain of human existence. The woman had been sick with a continual hemorrhage for twelve long years and no one could cure her. She had tried all sorts of treatments and had spent her money on every kind of doctor, but if anything had grown sicker instead of growing well. Perhaps by this time she secretly felt she was incurable, marked out for a lifetime of suffering. But she hadn't given up, she hadn't accepted the inevitable. She wasn't going to be a full-time invalid if she could help it.

The nature of her ailment was particularly degrading in the Israel of Jesus' day, because women with flows of blood were held to be "unclean," literally untouchable. So she really took her courage in her hands when she touched the garment of the great rabbi.

This may have been one of the reasons why she did not confront Jesus and ask for help. She was afraid of being rejected. Also, she may have had a certain timidity about committing herself to ask for the whole attention of this healer. She only wanted to touch the hem of his garment, so if it wasn't the right thing to do she wouldn't be held accountable or punished.

In asking "Who touched my garments?" Jesus made her stand up and be counted. He made her face up fully to her need to be healed. He asked for a full commitment from her. He didn't treat her like a child but like a mature person, responsible for her acts. Jesus knew he had healed her, but he wanted a face-to-face confrontation with her as a whole adult.

This woman with an issue of blood is a prototype of all sick women, yesterday and today. She had gone to all the physicians, but she needed skill and power beyond what they could offer. Jesus cured her when the doctors couldn't. The sickness may have been entirely physical; it may have had psychological roots beyond the physical manifestation. From the data given, we do not know, but we can tell that she was instantly healed by Christ's power.

Several characteristics beside her sickness stand out in this confrontation. In timidly touching the hem of Jesus' garment in the thick of the crowd, she reminds one of those who wish to be healed today but who don't want to get totally involved. They don't want their motivations and needs laid bare to the public eye. Sometimes they are afraid to commit themselves fully to a cause or to a community, because they are afraid their efforts may fail. Sometimes they are afraid to be claimed by anything outside of themselves. They want to be free of all commitments, even if it means bleeding alone.

This woman felt unworthy to claim the full attention of the

healer. Perhaps she felt she wasn't important enough or good enough to take his time, to ask for anything. Many women seem to have this approach. It is a deep, pervasive inferiority complex that undervalues their personhood and is devastating to the psyche. One of the reasons for this feeling today may be that in America we tend to measure everything by its economic worth. We evaluate people most of the time by how much money they make, rather than by their contribution to society, their intelligence, their capacity for love, or any other gauge. The majority of women are housewives and are not paid by a cash salary, so in the eyes of many they have no worth. If they have jobs, these jobs are often low paying, mechanical types of work. Or if they are fortunate enough to have a better job, they are usually paid less than a man doing the same work. Eventually they internalize this estimate of unworthiness and become cringing beggars, fearful to ask too much of society. In seeking health they merely touch the hem of the Savior's garment.

But Jesus did not judge by the world's standards. He saw the need and the worth of this woman, and he liberated her from sickness. He knew the need was real and he justified her hopes.

Not only did he heal her from her physical illness, but he released her from her fears and suffering, often concomitants of sickness but frequently existing by themselves. Sometimes the anxiety about oneself is a greater burden to bear than whatever is causing the anxiety. Jesus removed this burden of suffering.

Jesus also liberated this woman from her feelings of inferiority and unworthiness. He called her forth from her hiding place and confirmed her as a person. He acknowledged her faith and her determination.

And he called her out of passivity into activity in holding her responsible for her acts. He said in effect, "Don't feel unworthy and inferior; you are a person worthy to be healed, worthy to claim my attention. Stand up and acknowledge your personhood, your rights as a human being."

Betty Friedan has commented on the fact that so many women today crowd the offices of doctors and psychiatrists. She feels that many of their ailments are the product of buried anger and frustration with their lot as women. It is possible that the bleeding of the woman in the New Testament episode may be symbolic as well as physical. Certainly many women have metaphorically bled as a result of their treatment as women. Many have suffered wounds from the compound of denigration and servitude which the world holds out to them.

Part of the treatment of Jesus was to make the sick woman whole in body and in spirit. He acknowledged both her physical condition and her spiritual condition when he said, "Daughter, your faith has made you well; go in peace, and be healed of your disease." In an age in which the medical profession acknowledges the psychosomatic basis for many illnesses, this pronouncement strikes us as a profound insight into the nature of illness.

Jesus was interested in the whole person. He recognized that women could and should be whole beings, integrated and liberated in body and spirit. He didn't feel they were inferior people who had to approach him in a special, unobtrusive way. In his response to the timid gesture of the sick woman he demanded that she reveal her whole self and acknowledge her personhood and her responsibility. She was totally healed because he did not respond in a halfway fashion to her need. He called forth a whole self, a responsible human being from the woman who was sick. Her life from then on would be totally different. Not only was she well where she had been sick, but she was whole where she had been divided.

The healing of Jesus always worked upon the total person, not just one aspect or symptom. As with the paralytic to whom he said, "Your sins are forgiven you," he understood the spiritual causes and dimensions of sickness and suffering.

A long sickness such as the woman with the hemorrhage suffered can be a debilitating process, both for the patient and those around her—her family, friends, or caretakers. In the process the patient often becomes less of a person, almost a thing. Sympathy is easy at first, but as the ailment drags on year after year sympathy, tolerance, sometimes even humanity dry up for the one who is sick. We all imagine that our health is part of us when we have it, an essential component of our being. When sickness comes, especially a long, draining illness, we become half a person or almost a different person. We become subhuman without willing it in any way.

Through Christ's healing touch the woman with an issue of blood emerged from this captivity into a new existence. She was a well person; she was a whole person; she was a woman liberated from disease and division.

If women today could be healed of the divisions of their spirits, they would be liberated for a new, more meaningful existence. If society would come to a realistic assessment of the capabilities and potentialities of women, not as special cases but as human beings, instead of imposing roles and stereotypes on them, women would be released from their divided selves. Instead of being half persons and half some inferior domestic species they would be free to grow as human beings. It would be harder, it is true, to mount advertising campaigns based on infantile or adolescent motivations, and consumerism might suffer. But the wards of our medical and psychiatric hospitals would not be as full.

Our society does not have an answer to sickness. Even our hospitals are ailing, financially and in terms of personnel. They cannot provide the solutions to our many illnesses. But Jesus, in making people whole, pointed the way in which we should go.

7

The Foreigner

And behold, a Canaanite woman from that region came out and cried, "Have mercy on me, O Lord, Son of David; my daughter is severely possessed by a demon." But he did not answer her a word. And his disciples came and begged him, saying, "Send her away, for she is crying after us." He answered, "I was sent only to the lost sheep of the house of Israel." But she came and knelt before him, saying, "Lord, help me." And he answered, "It is not fair to take the children's bread and throw it to the dogs." She said, "Yes, Lord, yet even the dogs eat the crumbs that fall from their master's table." Then Jesus answered her, "O woman, great is your faith! Be it done for you as you desire." And her daughter was healed instantly.—Matthew 15:22–28

The first thing we are told about this importunate woman is that she is a foreigner. In the account of Mark (7:25–30) she is called a Syrophoenician; in Matthew she appears as a Canaanite.

And yet, despite her different origins, her concerns are the same as those of any mother: anxiety for her sick daughter. Her character is very plainly marked in this encounter. We are first impressed by her persistence—she kept after the disciples until she got to the healer, and she kept after Jesus until she gained her point. She didn't care if she was making a spectacle of herself. She continued crying out until she was heard. She wasn't tactful and ladylike in her request. She was so persistent that the disciples begged Jesus to send her away because she was making so much noise.

Her love for her child made her disregard what may have been the usual reticence of women's conduct. Her need drove her to Jesus to obtain healing for her daughter.

She was direct in her pleading for health for her child. When she came up against the officiousness of Christ's followers, it didn't stop her. Even when she came up against Jesus' initial denial, she persevered.

She used her intelligence and her wit to gain Christ's attention and to convince him that her need was real. Her courage and humor came to the fore when she dared to answer Jesus back on his own terms. And Jesus must have been impressed with her humility as well as her ready wit when she asked for the crumbs from the table. She was willing to give up her pride and her prestige for the sake of her child.

She also knew where salvation was. This knowledge communicated itself to Jesus, and he responded to her fully, not as a foreigner any longer but as a caring person.

The main point of this story is that the woman who appealed to Jesus was a foreigner. A difference in nationality does not mean that much to us today, but at the time of Jesus this placed her outside the normal channels of communication of the Israelites. The Jews were jealous of their identity as a people and were suspicious of those of backgrounds different than their own.

More than that, the Canaanite woman was under double jeopardy as an outsider—an outsider by race and an outsider by sex. Vivian Gornick in *Woman in Sexist Society* has defined woman as a perpetual outsider, and Simone de Beauvoir in *The Second Sex* names woman as "The Other." What is meant by this definition?

Women are not outsiders in their own homes. If anything, the man is occasionally made to feel like an outsider in domestic concerns. But when women leave their homes and go into the communities around them, they are often made to feel like outsiders, trespassers on the prerogatives of a man's world. Second-class citizenship is automatically conferred upon them, either in paid or volunteer work. They do the typing, envelope-stuffing, coffee-making, etc., that supports an executive structure. Often it is only by infinite tact and ability that their ideas are used in policy-making or other intelligent activity.

Some women, of course, make themselves outsiders. They are so accustomed to ruling a home and small children that they apply this attitude to the rest of the world and try to run every group they encounter like a happy nursery school. As other adults understandably resent being treated this way, the home ruler in the world soon becomes an outsider.

But many women are made to feel like outsiders simply because they are women. A woman recently met a man she knew in the center of the city at lunch time. He was astounded to see her. He said, "How come you're here and not home?" It was beyond his comprehension that an adult woman with a comfortable house in the suburbs might come into the metropolitan area for any reason.

It is, of course, ridiculous that more than one half the population should be made to feel like outsiders by the other half when they step out of their homes, but such is often the case. To be out of the house seems to be doing something meaningful and important and economically rewarding, and this is looked on by many, both men and women, as a male preserve. If a woman succeeds in accomplishing something in the outside world, she is often called "pushy" or "mannish" as a putdown to her ambitions.

The Canaanite woman was an outsider and she was definitely pushy. But she accomplished a great deal, not only in her own life, in the healing of her daughter, but also in the life of Christ. This foreign woman showed Jesus that his mission was not only to the lost sheep of the house of Israel but to the whole world. For her he was not only the promised Messiah for the Jews, a prophet in a line of prophets, but the Lord of all people. Jesus must have realized from her urgent appeal the universal needs of people, regardless of their nationalities. He saw a faith that was not conditioned by national characteristics and he responded to it.

This response had far-reaching results for the future of Christianity. Through Christ's acknowledgment of people outside Judaism, the groundwork for the inclusive character of Christianity was laid. The Canaanite or Syrophoenician woman was the first in a procession of outsiders which included Samaritans, tax collectors, a Roman centurion, and many others. She marked out the unlimited nature of Christ's relation to his followers; female and male, sick and well, all kinds, colors, and nations. The future of Christianity lay in its appeal to all strata of society and in its availability to all. Christian acceptance is not exclusive but inclusive. It cannot be an exclusive club for the "Right People" if it truly follows a man who said he came not to the righteous but to sinners who needed him more.

Jesus had been trained in the tradition of the Hebraic tradition of a Messiah. This Messiah was to come to the Jews alone and lead them to great things. Some groups even believed he would be a national savior that would free Israel from Roman rule. Others postulated that the coming Messiah would be a direct descendant from King David and would help regain Israel's lost glories. Jesus conceived of his mission in broader terms and saw it in relation to a kingdom not of this world, but in the early days of his ministry he seems to have believed he was sent to save Israel only.

The appeal of the Canaanite woman and her faith in him transcended all the boundaries he had known. This encounter with her may have changed his understanding of his mission completely. Through her he recognized that the traditional view of the Messiah was too narrow. By her courage, intelligence, and persistence she enlarged the dimensions of his vision. Jesus discovered that the boundaries of men were artificial, and that the needs of all humanity were his province. The outsider was an outsider no more.

8

The Samaritan Woman at the Well

There came a woman of Samaria to draw water. Jesus said to her, "Give me a drink." For his disciples had gone away into the city to buy food. The Samaritan woman said to him, "How is it that you, a Jew, ask a drink of me, a woman of Samaria?" For Jews have no dealings with Samaritans. Jesus answered her, "If you knew the gift of God, and who it is that is saying to you, 'Give me a drink,' you would have asked him, and he would have given you living water." The woman said to him, "Sir, you have nothing to draw with, and the well is deep; where do you get that living water?" . . . Jesus said to her, "Every one who drinks of this water will thirst again, but whoever drinks of the water that I shall give him will never thirst; the water that I shall give him will become in him a spring of water welling up to eternal life." The woman said to him, "Sir, give me this water, that I may not thirst, nor come here to draw."

Jesus said to her, "Go, call your husband, and come here." The woman answered him, "I have no husband." Jesus said to her, "You are right in saying, 'I have no husband'; for you have had five husbands, and he whom you now have is not your husband; this you said truly." The woman said to him, "Sir, I perceive that you are a prophet. . . . I know that Messiah is coming (he who is called Christ); when he comes, he will show us all things." Jesus said to her, "I who speak to you am he."

Just then his disciples came. They marveled that he was talking with a woman, but none said, "What do you wish?" or, "Why are you talking with her?" So the woman left her water jar, and went away into the city, and said to the people, "Come, see a man who told me all that I ever did. Can this be the Christ?" They went out of the city and were coming to him.—John 4:7–11, 13–19, 25–30

This episode took place at Jacob's well by the town of Sychar in Samaria. At this time the Jews treated the Samaritans as aliens because after the exile the people of Israel who had stayed in Samaria intermarried with Assyrians. In the Jews' eyes this made the stock impure, and they refused the help of the Samaritans in building the temple at Jerusalem. The Samaritans then built their own temple on Mount Gerizim and the split was complete. The situation was further aggravated in the time of Jesus because Samaritans mistreated Jewish pilgrims going to Jerusalem who crossed their territory, and the Jews rejected Samaritans as Levitically unclean and avoided them whenever possible. For the Jews, Samaritans were a debased people and occupied the lowest rung on the social and economic totem pole. In modern terms the Jewish rejection of the Samaritans as equals has been likened to the white racist rejection of the black people. From this point of view, the encounter of Christ with the Samaritan woman could be seen as the equivalent of a confrontation with a black woman of today.

Typically, Jesus was not moved by the prejudices of his day against either Samaritans or women, nor was he contained by contemporary categories. He moved toward the woman in his natural request for water.

She, on the other hand, was defensive at first and concerned with the technicalities of the relationship. Or it is possible that in her first question she was mocking him slightly about his need for water which was so great that he had to ask a rejected member of humanity, a Samaritan woman, for it.

But she soon discovered that it was her need, not his, that Jesus was leading to when he spoke of the water of eternal life.

When she wanted to hear more, Jesus told her to get her husband to come and listen with her. This may have been a prudent idea, because it would have protected Jesus from any accusation of seduction. However, it seems more likely that it was a move on the part of Jesus to get the woman to open up the reality of her life. Even when he revealed his knowledge of her circumstances, she still fought the battle to keep the encounter from getting too deep, too close to her defenses. She asked him a theological question about worship as a proper bit of conventional conversation with a prophet.

Jesus transcended the technicalities of her question and the religious practices of the Samaritans and Jews by opening up the vast scope of true worship. Then the Samaritan woman sensed that this man might indeed be the promised Messiah, the Christ who was to come. And Jesus fulfilled her expectation by revealing to her, "I who speak to you am he."

What kind of woman was this woman by the well to whom Jesus communicated his messiahship? First of all, it must be admitted that she was a woman of experience. She had had five husbands and had a present lover. She may have been a beautiful woman, who expected and received the homage of men and the jealousy of women. Her approach to Jesus may have been mildly flirtatious in her first question of him. It is hard to judge, because although the Bible gives us the words it doesn't tell us the tone of voice.

The Samaritan woman would seem to have had a great deal of experience with men and with the world, but she was still looking for fulfillment. She had not found it in her relationship to the men in her past or in her present. She was intelligent and searching, and in Christ's response to her she found the answer for her life.

One thing in the narrative is evident: she was a person, not just a shadow. We don't know her name, but her presence as an individual with ready wit and an inquiring mind is clearly felt. It is interesting in this context that Jesus frequently seemed to prefer women who used their minds, who were themselves, and who thought and acted outside the traditional expectations of their culture. He could and did relate to persons rather than to stereotypes, and he encouraged the women he met to go beyond the confines of second-class citizenship.

In the meeting with Jesus the Samaritan woman made a journey from legalism to authenticity. She started with the outer, conventional forms of things and ended with an inner conviction that Jesus was the Messiah, both to the world and to her life. She went through a transformation in her life and in her perception of life.

This transformation made her the second woman missionary for Jesus. She left what she was doing and went to bring the people of the city to Jesus. People believed in Jesus because of the woman's testimony, and many asked him to remain at Sychar. He stayed for two days and brought still more Samaritans to an understanding of God through his words. As he said of what the Samaritan woman was accomplishing, "I tell you, lift up your eyes, and see how the fields are already white for harvest. He who reaps receives wages, and gathers fruit for eternal life, so that sower and reaper may rejoice together (John 4:35–36)."

This encounter of Jesus with the woman of Samaria exposes many facets of his attitude and ministry. In the first place, Jesus broke through rabbinical taboos to address this woman. As the law of the time decreed, "A man should hold no conversation with a woman in the streets, not even with his own wife, lest men should gossip." [1] This prevailing view was reflected in his disciples' attitude when they returned from buying food and "marveled that he was talking with a woman." But Jesus was not limited by the customs of his day in his approach to life, and he addressed the woman at the well as an equal, a potential sharer in the kingdom of God. He recognized her intelligence, her eagerness for the water of eternal life, and her great ability as a communicator of the good news.

Jesus didn't preach "at" the woman; he related to her life. He wasn't interested in discussing theological theories; he was engrossed by the essence of religion and its relation to people's needs. He told the woman that God could not be confined to one place or one people or even one sex. God is beyond matter and available to all.

Finally, it was in this meeting with a woman that Jesus publicly revealed his messiahship. In some ways she was the least likely person to whom to tell this portentous news. She was leading an irregular life, she came from a minority and rejected group, and she was a member of that neglected category—womankind. And yet, it was this woman who elicited from Jesus his public proclamation that he was the chosen one of Israel.

It is highly significant that women occupied such a pivotal position in the ministry of Jesus. The Canaanite woman revealed to him that his ministry was not just to the lost sheep of the house of Israel but to the whole world. The Samaritan woman drew forth from Jesus the acknowledgment that he was indeed the Messiah, and she acted on this news at once by bringing the whole community to him. It is possible that she too was a catalyst in Jesus' full realization of the dimensions of his mission and his ministry. His statements to the disciples about his work after the conversation with her show this clearly: "I have food to eat of which you do not know. . . . My food is to do the will of him who sent me, and to accomplish his work (John 4:32, 34)." This is the first time in the Gospel of John that Jesus identified himself specifically as the Messiah and acted on this recognition.

There is another strand in this account of the Samaritan woman, a strand of turning again in her life. She had to accept the facts of her life as they were and to become open to new possibilities. The root meaning of the word repentance is turning again. The Samaritan woman turned from her former life to the vision of the life Jesus showed her.

Today repentance seems to be an obscure virtue. People feel that repentance is gloomy, depressing, and probably even neurotic. There are so few standards from which to transgress that the process of penitence becomes obsolete. Lenten hymns which explore the depths of sorrow and forgiveness are discarded in favor of more cheerful tunes so that no one may be disturbed.

But we are in the midst of disturbing times whether we like it or not, and trying to mask the upheaval and distress by nonoffensive hymns and prayers in the church does not meet the problem. Women and men are still subject to temptation, transgression, and self-indulgence whether they recognize it in formal terms or not. The culture in general no longer tries to judge conduct by Christian standards, but, strangely enough, the effects of falling short of Christian goals are the same. Lives become disrupted by selfishness, indulgence, inhumanity, jealousy, anger, envy, lust, and all the traditional seven deadly sins. The names may be different but the effects are still devastating, both in one's own life and the lives of others.

This is why Christianity has reckoned with human shortcomings and perversity and provided a way out for the alienated through recognition, repentance, and forgiveness. There is no way to reconciliation and wholeness without a turning from past behavior to new life. The Samaritan woman discovered this when she turned from her past and a whole new life and purpose opened up for her. She turned again after realizing her turning away.

In one way this whole incident is a parable about the renewal of life. There is the symbolic presence of the woman at the well and the reference to the water of eternal life. Water has always been a metaphor of baptism, for regeneration and rebirth. The story points to the way in which Jesus renews our lives by offering us the living water of faith. It shows how an episode in daily life can be transformed into a new understanding of life and its challenges.

Jesus didn't structure the encounter with the woman at the well to suit his purposes. He let it unfold to its proper and inevitable conclusion. Jesus didn't enter situations with set expectations. He related to things as they were, not as he wanted them to be. Some of his greatest revelations appear to come in moments of quiet encounter or reflection.

Jesus seemed to be learning about his mission as he met life. In his openness to people around him, especially women, he came to understand the essential character of humanity, its needs and its possibilities. Women were often the catalysts in this process.

The woman of Samaria has her counterpart in women today who have had much experience but are still looking for something to fulfill their lives. Sometimes they run through a series of emotional attachments and emerge bitter and disillusioned. Many times they become servants of causes which attract them but do not satisfy their search or use their talents truly. If they are fortunate they meet the one who is waiting for them at the well of life, waiting to renew and transform their existence.

9

Widows

> And he sat down opposite the treasury, and watched the multitude putting money into the treasury. Many rich people put in large sums. And a poor widow came, and put in two copper coins, which make a penny. And he called his disciples to him, and said to them, "Truly, I say to you, this poor widow has put in more than all those who are contributing to the treasury. For they all contributed out of their abundance; but she out of her poverty has put in everything she had, her whole living."—Mark 12:41–44

This is one of several stories told in the New Testament about widows. It usually goes by the title "The Widow's Mite" and illustrates, as many of the comparisons that Jesus made, that it is the intention that is important in an act, not the actual amount involved. Jesus always looked at the inner revelation in attitude and event rather than their outer or seeming appearance.

Jesus had a special concern for widows. In the Israel of his day widows were discriminated against. They wore special black clothing to mark their bereaved state. Unlike a widow in many other cultures, under Hebraic law she did not inherit from her husband. One reason for this neglect may be that the Jews believed that death before old age was a terrible calamity, possibly a judgment for sins committed, and the wife was included in this judgment. Thus being a widow meant not only bereavement and deprivation, but disgrace.[1] Isaiah spells this out precisely:

Fear not, for you will not be ashamed;
  be not confounded, for you will
    not be put to shame;
for you will forget the shame of your youth,
  and the reproach of your widowhood
    you will remember no more.
For your Maker is your husband,
  the Lord of hosts is his name;
and the Holy One of Israel is your Redeemer,
  the God of the whole earth he is called.
For the Lord has called you
  like a wife forsaken and grieved
    in spirit,
like a wife of youth when she is cast off,
  says your God.
For a brief moment I forsook you,
  but with great compassion I will gather you.
In overflowing wrath for a moment
  I hid my face from you,
but with everlasting love I will have
    compassion on you,
    says the Lord, your Redeemer.—Isaiah 54:4–8

This passage refers to God's relationship to Israel as a nation but also includes the special relationship and care of the redeemer of Israel for the widowed woman in her grief and loss which Jesus himself embodied.

Burdened with the reproach of widowhood the Hebrew woman also lost much of her authority and well-being in society on the death of her husband. At this time the eldest son inherited his father's goods and took over the management of the house. If the widow was childless, she usually returned to her father's house.

There was the Hebrew law of levirate marriage which held that the widow could be married to the next youngest unmarried brother of her husband so as to keep her cared for by her husband's family. However, many times no brothers were available, or the man might refuse to perform this function. Then the widow was left without economic security, not to speak of emotional satisfactions or social acceptance.

Basically, the status of the widow in the Hebraic community reveals the terrible bias of a patriarchal society where women are considered chattels and breeders, not independent individuals or persons. The idea of passing a wife from brother to brother is as repugnant in its lack of choice for the widow as is her being cast out on her husband's death with little economic provision and few talents or opportunities to earn a living on her own.

Widows were preeminently a disadvantaged group in the social circle of Jesus' day. He recognized their suffering as outcasts and responded to it as he responded to all those rejected by society. He knew their vulnerability, testified to by the Deuteronomic laws in which the Levite, the sojourner, the fatherless, and the widow are to be given a tithe of the produce (Deuteronomy 26:12). Widows lived by public compassion and generosity. They were the gleaners of the community, as Ruth, an earlier widow, had gleaned the grain left for her by the harvesters.

And yet, the widow who received so little from men was willing to give to God. Jesus calls attention to the "givingness" of the widow in spite of the harsh conditions of her life. He appreciated this extraordinary gratitude which came from so little and gave so much.

Because of her vulnerable condition, the widow was often oppressed by men taking advantage of her situation. Jesus was following in the footsteps of the prophetic tradition in his concern for the widow's state. Isaiah said:

> Woe to those who decree iniquitous decrees,
>   and the writers who keep writing oppression,
> to turn aside the needy from justice
>   and to rob the poor of my people
>   of their right,
> that widows may be their spoil,
>   and that they may make the
>   fatherless their prey!—Isaiah 10:1–2

Malachi denounced "those who oppress the hireling in his wages, the widow and the orphan (Mal. 3:5)." The prophets condemned those who made a victim of the unprotected widow. Jesus went one step farther: he held the widow up as an example to the society which had rejected or belittled her.

Jesus responded even more directly to the plight of the widow in his encounter with the widow of Nain.

> Soon afterward he went to a city called Nain, and his disciples and a great crowd went with him. As he drew near to the gate of the city, behold, a man who had died was being carried out, the only son of his mother, and she was a widow; and a large crowd from the city was with her. And when the Lord saw her, he had compassion on her and said to her, "Do not weep." And he came and touched the bier, and the bearers stood still. And he said, "Young man, I say to you, arise." And the dead man sat up, and began to speak. And he gave him to his mother.—Luke 7:11–15

The grief of this mother must have been almost too great to bear. First her husband had died and then her only son, now a young man, had also perished. She had lost two persons she loved and had probably lost her livelihood as well.

Jesus did not murmur words of comfort only. His understanding and pity were transformed into drastic action as he brought the son to life. The widow's deep sorrow called forth an extraordinary act of compassion and restoration.

It may be that Jesus had a special awareness of the widow's situation, as it has been suggested that his mother, Mary, was by this time a widow. There is no mention of Joseph in the Gospels after the visit to the temple when Jesus was twelve years old, and some authorities have conjectured that Jesus did not start his public ministry until he was about thirty years old because of his responsibility to his mother. Whether this interpretation is true or not, Jesus always showed himself sensitive to the needs of widows and understood the difficulties and deprivations of their condition. He reached out with both hands to restore what circumstances and custom had taken from them.

Today the condition of widows is, in most cases, much better than it was in the days of Jesus. Most societies do not exclude widows from inheritance; in fact, the majority insist that a man's wife be provided for. Insurance usually covers much of her cost of living, and social security benefits add to her livelihood.

But there is another side to the story. As Simone de Beauvoir remarked in an article on old age in *Life* magazine in the spring of 1972, people avoid looking at the problems of the elderly because it is too difficult. The same holds true for the problems of widowhood. It is too painful to encounter the difficulties involved with the loss of a husband.

First, there is a terrible sense of loss when the man whom a woman has chosen to live her life with dies. It spells the terminus of her hopes and expectations of a normal, sharing life. Unless she is an unusually independent person she will feel lost, perhaps even guilty for not being able to avert the catastrophe.

Besides her own life alone, she must face the responsibility of bringing up her children, if she has any, without a father. It is usually a difficult job for two active concerned parents to bring up their children, and when a person faces it alone the task is awesome.

As a widow, a woman is frequently discriminated against socially. At one extreme she is excluded from parties as a single woman in a coupled society; at the other reach, much to her embarrassment, her friends may try constantly to play matchmaker. Then there are men who feel that widowhood makes a woman an easy sexual mark, one who is grateful for any sort of "consolation."

In addition to all this, although our society has conditioned us to think of the rich widow, many widows are poor. Among deprived classes the husband has no money and often no insurance to leave. Social security provides only a pittance and the widow must work to support her family. She is not only legally and socially the head of the family but is its economic provider as well. How well can she support her family under these circumstances? As a woman she is discriminated against by the economic establishment, earns less than a man (often for the same job), and usually has less of a chance at jobs commensurate with her talents. In some extraordinary cases, as with Sen. Maurine Newburger, she takes over her husband's job. But this is the exception, not the rule, and usually occurs in cases where the need is not that pressing economically. Many widows are oppressed economically and socially today in a society that does not really try to understand and help.

One place that widows are accepted and encouraged is in the life of the church. In spite of Noah's ark, this institution does not go on a two-by-two social schedule, and the contribution a widow can make to its life is much appreciated. The service of a widow in teaching, serving on governing boards and vestries, listening and helping sustains many a church and is felt by many of its members. Ideally, the church should be able to give of its life to widows as well as receive of their talents. If widows have sought a refuge and a reciprocation in churches this is not surprising, as Jesus recognized and pointed out in the Gospels their great capacity for unselfish giving. It may have been that many of the women who followed him in Judea were widows. They listened to his words and ministered to the needs of the disciples. They had found someone who considered them not as outcasts but as examples to the world. They discovered a person who suffered with them in their loss and who opened a new way of life for them.

10

Martha
of Bethany

Now as they went on their way, he entered a village; and a woman named Martha received him into her house. And she had a sister called Mary, who sat at the Lord's feet and listened to his teaching. But Martha was distracted with much serving; and she went to him and said, "Lord, do you not care that my sister has left me to serve alone? Tell her then to help me." But the Lord answered her, "Martha, Martha, you are anxious and troubled about many things; one thing is needful. Mary has chosen the good portion, which shall not be taken away from her."—Luke 10:38–42

This is the picture we get of Martha: the anxious, bustling housewife, concerned that everything be in order for Jesus' visit. Many commentators interpret her role as being the older sister since the house belonged to her, and Mary and Lazarus, her sister and brother, were probably younger than Martha. It would seem that the ordering of the household devolved on Martha, and she accepted it as her responsibility.

The interpretation of Martha's character depends on whether we see her busy over needless work, extra fussy about details; or whether she is, as others picture her, a strong, efficient, reliable person, contributing to her family and her society. In this case, Martha would be taking a responsible role in the care of her house while Mary seems only concerned with herself.

Our view should hinge on our interpretation of Christ's remark.

Was Martha busy about too many things that were *not* needful? Had she lost herself in housework and the caring for things instead of people? Jesus certainly seems to infer this. He was more interested in communicating with her as a person than in seeing a spotless house or being served a seven-course dinner.

Christ's remark, "You are busy about *many* things but Mary has found the *one* thing needful," could point to the fact that Martha was encumbered with meaningless trivia but did not grasp the one thing necessary to her salvation—finding herself as a person. She needed to be able to be quiet long enough to really relate to her guest and hear what he was saying.

Jesus may have been warning Martha not to be limited by the world of her own small house and its narrow range but to look beyond its confines, both mental and spiritual. Martha was like too many women who become involved in housekeeping tasks and who are burdened by unnecessary housepride. They need to see beyond the limitations of this small, task-centered world and to imagine themselves in some role other than domestic servant.

Jesus appears to be the first man in history who didn't expect to be waited on hand and foot. He obviously didn't think that women's place was in the kitchen or serving him. He did not put Martha in the role of a domestic servant but rather as a sharing, participating equal. The implications of this are revolutionary. The personhood of woman is removed from a narrow stereotype of domestic service, housewife, housekeeper, nurse, and is freed to become an independent being, ready to share with man in a one-to-one relationship.

This does not mean that women should immediately abandon all housework. But needless tasks can be eliminated, many things can be simplified, work can be shared by all members of the family, and it becomes less a burden and constant concern. Freeing ourselves from housepride also means freeing ourselves from constantly comparing our household with our neighbor's: Is our house as neat as theirs? Do we have dinners that are as elaborate and meet their gourmet standards? Will we be judged on the quantity of our possessions or the whiteness of our wash? Jesus liberates us from this kind of one-upmanship in housekeeping which can deprive us of personhood, wholeness, and receptivity to others.

The story of raising Lazarus in the Gospel of John sheds further light on the character of Martha.

Now a certain man was ill, Lazarus of Bethany, the village of Mary and her sister Martha. . . . So the sisters sent to him, saying, "Lord, he whom you love is ill." But when Jesus heard it he said, "This illness is not unto death; it is for the glory of God, so that the Son of God may be glorified by means of it."

Now Jesus loved Martha and her sister and Lazarus. So when he heard that he was ill, he stayed two days longer in the place where he was. Then after this he said to the disciples, "Let us go into Judea again." . . . Thus he spoke, and then he said to them, "Our friend Lazarus has fallen asleep, but I go to awake him out of sleep." The disciples said to him, "Lord, if he has fallen asleep, he will recover." Then Jesus told them plainly, "Lazarus is dead; and for your sake I am glad that I was not there, so that you may believe. But let us go to him." . . .

Now when Jesus came, he found that Lazarus had already been in the tomb four days. Bethany was near Jerusalem, about two miles off, and many of the Jews had come to Martha and Mary to console them concerning their brother. When Martha heard that Jesus was coming, she went and met him, while Mary sat in the house. Martha said to Jesus, "Lord, if you had been here, my brother would not have died. And even now I know that whatever you ask from God, God will give you." Jesus said to her, "Your brother will rise again." Martha said to him, "I know that he will rise again in the resurrection at the last day." Jesus said to her, "I am the resurrection and the life; he who believes in me, though he die, yet shall he live, and whoever lives and believes in me shall never die. Do you believe this?" She said to him, "Yes, Lord; I believe that you are the Christ, the son of God, he who is coming into the world."

When she had said this, she went and called her sister Mary, saying quietly, "The Teacher is here and is calling for you." And when she heard it, she rose quickly and went to him. Now Jesus had not yet come to the village, but was still in the place where Martha had met him. . . . When Jesus saw her weeping, and the Jews who came with her also weeping, he was deeply moved in spirit and troubled; and he said, "Where have you laid him?" They said to him, "Lord, come and see." Jesus wept. So the Jews said, "See how he loved him!" But some of them said, "Could not he who opened the eyes of the blind man have kept this man from dying?"

Then Jesus, deeply moved again, came to the tomb; it was a cave, and a stone lay upon it. Jesus said, "Take away the stone." Martha, the sister of the dead man, said to him, "Lord, by this time there will be an odor, for he has been dead four days." Jesus said to her, "Did I not tell you that if you would believe you would see the glory of God?" So they took away the stone. And Jesus lifted up his eyes and said, "Father, I thank thee that thou hast heard me. I knew that thou hearest me always, but I have said this on account of the people standing by, that they may believe that thou didst send me." When he had said this, he cried with a loud voice, "Lazarus, come out." The dead man came out, his hands and feet bound with bandages, and his face wrapped with a cloth. Jesus said to them, "Unbind him, and let him go."—John 11:1, 3–7, 11–12, 14–15, 17–30, 33–44

Here some of the depths of Martha's personality emerge. As soon as Jesus comes, she goes to meet him. She shows herself to be active and vigorous in her approach. At first she does not understand when Jesus tells her that her brother will rise again. She thinks he is referring to the doctrine propounded by the Sadducees concerning a general resurrection on the last day or day of judgment. Jesus enlightens her: "I am the resurrection and the life; he who believes in me, though he die, yet shall he live, and whoever lives and believes in me shall never die." Here Jesus reveals the full quality of his ministry to Martha, and she understands that Jesus is really the ultimate savior for this life and the next. Jesus has revealed to a woman the secret of deliverance from the death of the spirit.

Martha does not keep this to herself. She goes at once to bring her grieving sister to Jesus.

When the party reaches the tomb and Jesus orders the stone to be rolled away, Martha's old practical character asserts itself. The

King James version of the Bible puts her response very baldly: "Lord, by this time he stinketh: for he hath been dead four days."

Martha is bound by the categories of this world; it is very hard for her to see beyond them. But when Lazarus comes forth, she recognizes Christ as the lord of life and death and perhaps realizes that everything in life is not ordered, controllable, and inevitable.

Mary
of Bethany

11

And she had a sister called Mary, who sat at the Lord's feet and listened to his teaching.—Luke 10:39

Mary of Bethany is not the easiest character in the world to know. She is quiet, intellectual, inward-looking, and completely engrossed in the teaching of Jesus. She does not fit easily into any stereotype of women, and much of our understanding of her as a person depends on our interpretation of the biblical story.

Mary is usually seen as a pendant to Martha, a diametrically opposed character. Where Martha is active and bustling, Mary appears contemplative in spirit. Martha's approach to the world is one of common sense, while Mary's is more emotional and poetic. Martha is always practical, whether it is in serving dinner or dealing with a corpse. Mary, on the other hand, appears more idealistic, looking for the reality behind the manifestations of the world. Martha is mundane in her considerations; Mary appears to exist on a more spiritual plane. We see Martha always talking, while Mary is usually listening. Martha is busy with all the concerns of daily life; Mary is reposeful. Martha could be called an other-directed person in comparison to Mary who seems to be more inner-directed.

Martha's temperament suits her to be a responsible housewife, while Mary appears to be something more. It has been pointed out that Martha took the typical woman's role, whereas Mary is seen in the "male role" of discipleship in listening to Christ's teaching.[1]

Although the temperaments of Martha and Mary were different in many ways, there were also striking similarities. The first quality that these two sisters shared was that they both loved and respected Jesus, and Jesus loved both of them. Both were also devoted to their brother Lazarus and were concerned about his welfare. Although much is made about the difference in responsibilities of these women in the household, it seems obvious that both probably helped in the work of the house. Martha's question to Jesus— "Lord, do you not care that my sister has left me to serve alone? Tell her then to help me"—would indicate that she was accustomed to Mary's help and in this instance was being deprived of it.

Martha has been represented as a selfless person concerned over the needs of others and Mary as concerned only with herself. This is not how Jesus saw it. He found in Mary a true sharer, one more concerned with learning about the kingdom of God than with worrying about outward trappings. As he said, "Mary has chosen the good portion, which shall not be taken from her." He refused to put her into a narrow stereotype of womanhood and saw her as a true person instead.

Mary, in other words, was very much an individual, not a role. She was as unique and various as any individual might be and could not be limited by set characteristics.

She was a person of rare perception. She understood the one thing needful instead of being anxious and troubled about many things as Martha was. Women become distracted so easily with the little things and minor matters that are not important in the long run. Their energies and talents become divided and are often squandered. Mary was single-minded in her quest for salvation.

Jesus appreciated Mary not as a servant or a housekeeper or even as a good listener, but rather as a person who could share as an equal. Mary never got hung up on the "woman's role" or "making men comfortable" or being charming and gracious only. Jesus treated her as a person and she responded by being one. One feels that if Jesus could have picked an earthly home, it would have been the one in Bethany.

More about the character of Mary is shown in the story of her anointing Jesus which appears in the Gospel of John.

> Six days before the Passover, Jesus came to Bethany, where Lazarus was, whom Jesus had raised from the dead. There they made him a supper; Martha served, but Lazarus was one of those at table with him. Mary took a pound of costly ointment of pure nard and anointed the feet of Jesus and wiped his feet with her hair; and the house was filled with the fragrance of the ointment.—John 12:1–3

The story goes on to tell of Judas Iscariot's protest that the money spent on the ointment should have been given to the poor, and Jesus replies that Mary should keep the rest of the ointment for the day of his burial.

This act of love on the part of Mary has been interpreted in various ways: as a royal anointing, as a preparation for burial, and as an extravagant gesture or possibly even a repentance for sins. One confusion caused by the story is that each of the Gospels tells it a little differently. The story as recorded in John is the only one which identifies Mary of Bethany with the anointing. In Luke 7:36–50 the woman anointing Jesus in the Pharisee's house is a sinner of whom Jesus says, "Her sins, which are many, are forgiven, for she loved much."

In the Gospels of John and Luke the feet of Jesus are anointed, whereas in the Gospels of Matthew and Mark (Matthew 26:6–13 and Mark 14:3–9) the head of Christ is anointed. The consensus of scholarly opinion appears to be that there were two different anointings, the Lucan version describing a repentant sinner's action and the accounts in Mark, Matthew, and John relating another anointing in which Mary of Bethany figured.

The two anointings have led to a supposition that if the sinner mentioned by Luke in the anointing story can be identified as Mary Magdalene, and if the anointing is also the one performed by Mary of Bethany, then possibly Mary Magdalene and Mary of Bethany are the same person. As the *Interpreter's Dictionary of the Bible* succinctly puts this tradition:

> The identification of Mary Magdalene, the sinner of Luke 7:36–50, and Mary of Bethany, widely accepted in the Western church from about the sixth century (but rejected in the Eastern), probably arose

because of the similarities in the stories of the anointing of Jesus by women contained in Luke 7:36–50, John 12:1–8, and the unfounded supposition that Mary Magdalene's "seven demons" were demons of unchastity.[2]

The weakness of this hypothesis is self-evident since none of the "ifs" are tenable. It is fairly clear that there were two separate anointings, and that Mary Magdalene was not the sinner mentioned in Luke 7:36–50. Not only that, but Mary of Bethany and Mary Magdalene are women of totally different experience and character. Mary of Bethany led a somewhat sheltered life at home with her sister and brother and was a thoughtful, quiet person, while Mary Magdalene appears to have lived in the world and to have been a somewhat flamboyant, emotional character. Mary Magdalene is never mentioned with Martha or Lazarus. Each of the women lived in totally different places: one in the village of Bethany, two miles east of Jerusalem; the other was from the town of Magdala, which is identified as Megdel, three miles northwest of Tiberias. In view of these completely different facts about the two women, one wonders if the tradition connecting the two, which grew up in the ascetic period of the church, may not have been an attempt to discredit Mary of Bethany and to make all the independent women who appear with Jesus notorious sinners. In this way the magnanimity of Jesus' behavior with women could be explained as pity rather than the revolutionary doctrine of equality.

For the Marys of today the message of Jesus is clear. His acceptance, even preference of Mary is an encouragement to the woman who wants to be more than a housewife and who wants to develop talents in other directions. Christ didn't ask women to hide their brains or their abilities. He asked them to be fully, honestly themselves. Women have been told to disguise their intelligence and to act like a birdbrain because men prefer them that way. On the contrary, intellectual, thoughtful men respond to intelligent women. Insecure men sometimes reject able women as a threat to their power, but if there was one thing Jesus wasn't, it was insecure.

In his encounters with Mary of Bethany, Jesus reveals the importance of a relationship between people, not just a constant busyness, always doing but seldom truly sharing. He appreciated Mary's entering into the depths of a relationship rather than just skimming over the surface.

In many ways Mary of Bethany seemed to be the ideal woman as far as Jesus was concerned. She was the one who knew the one thing needful. She wasn't distracted by trivia. In the last analysis she emerges as a real person of reciprocity and depth, of mind and spirit, of receiving and giving.

12

Mary Magdalene

And it came to pass afterward, that he went throughout every city and village, preaching and shewing the glad tidings of the kingdom of God: and the twelve *were* with him, and certain women, which had been healed of evil spirits and infirmities, Mary called Magdalene, out of whom went seven devils.—Luke 8:1–2, KJV

What was Mary Magdalene like? Who was she really?

There are two main traditions about her, depending on the interpretation of casting out seven demons. The older tradition finds its roots in the Talmud which mentions the fact that Magdala, the town which Mary came from and which is significantly associated with her name, was famed for its harlotry, and the vicious living there was so notorious that the town was destroyed by the Romans. If Mary Magdalene was associated with a town famous for its prostitutes, it is easy to assume that she was a prostitute also, and that the demons cast out were sins of evil living.

Another source of the identification of Mary Magdalene with the sins of the flesh has been the story of the woman anointing Christ's feet with ointment at the house of Simon the Leper, which comes directly before the introduction of Mary Magdalene in the Gospel of Luke (7:36–50). Here the woman in question is called a sinner, and it is implied by the reactions of the Pharisees that she was a prostitute. However, since Luke later names Mary Magdalene directly with the disciples, it seems strange that if the woman at the house of Simon the Leper was the same person as Mary Magdalene, he does not say so.

The tradition of Mary Magdalene as a prostitute has reaped a rich harvest of images in art and in literature. The picture of the Repent-ant Magdalene, all golden hair and tears as one critic so penetrat-ingly put it, sums up the dual strains of sensuality and asceticism, particularly in the baroque age. What a need mankind seems to have for the glamorous sinner!

If Mary Magdalene was indeed a prostitute, as some of the other women whom Jesus encountered were, she is a convincing example of his forgiveness for all conditions of humanity. Jesus understood the drives of hunger and poverty which forced women into prostitu-tion or the sensuality which led them to choose it. In forgiving them he restored their self-respect and respect for their own bodies so that they would not continue being used by men. There was no condemnation in his "Go and sin no more"; only a releasing of the women from their past to lead a new life.

In Israel during the first century, poverty drove many women into prostitution. It was one of the few ways that they could earn a living. Other careers were not open to them, lacking as they were in education and social acceptance. Some may have become prostitutes from choice because they "loved much," but from their tears it would not seem that they found much happiness in this life.

Prostitution is not a thing of the past only; right now poverty and need still force women into this degrading occupation. Unlike the stereotype of the glamorous call girl or the well-dressed Times Square hooker, the average prostitute works because of poverty. This poverty is sometimes so extreme that there are cases like the thirteen-year-old Harlem girl with a mother on drugs, who took to the street to get food for her younger brothers and sisters. For street prostitutes the total loss of humanity and the lack of choice make these women objects who prey upon and are preyed upon by men.

In contemporary society, love affairs and temporary sexual liai-sons are now entered into most casually by many women, but often they find they cannot use their bodies as machines for gratification without involvement. They also discover that their genuine giving can be misused by their lovers, and they become objects of easy pleasure to men and nothing more. Their personhood is completely denied: they are no more than a category.

Contemporary movies such as *McCabe and Mrs. Miller* present organized prostitution in a brothel as all one warm, happy family with lots of laughs, but the truth of the situation is much nearer to the portraits by Toulouse-Lautrec of desperate, degenerate, and alienated women.

Romantic as the portrayal of Mary Magdalene as a prostitute may be, contemporary biblical criticism points out that it is more probable that the possession by seven devils referred to the concept of mental illness in the Israel of Christ's time. Mary Magdalene was possibly a multiple schizophrenic, who had been cured by Jesus in the same way as he had cast out demons from the Gerasene demoniac (Luke 8:26–39). The term "possessed by demons" was the way the Jews explained the confusion and mental strife of the multiple schizophrenic. It is easy to imagine how Jesus banished the many possessions and ambivalences of conflicting spirits by pointing to the one true way. Instead of Mary Magdalene being at war with herself, she became the follower of the man who was truly her savior and her deliverer from mental darkness. She became integrated into a whole person after her encounter with Jesus.

The term identity crisis is prevalent in current jargon. It describes the doubts about who we really are and the strivings to find direction as individuals. We seem to have many possible roles we could play; we have worn so many masks we no longer know who we are as real people. Mary Magdalene may have been pulled in various directions by similar "demons" before she met Jesus. He freed her to find herself.

It is highly significant that the Gospels of Matthew, Mark, and John tell of Mary Magdalene and other women watching the crucifixion.

There were also women looking on from afar, among whom were Mary Magdalene, and Mary the mother of James the younger and of Joses, and Salome, who, when he was in Galilee, followed him, and ministered to him; and also other women who came up with him to Jerusalem.—Mark 15:40–41

But, except for the "disciple whom he loved" mentioned in the Gospel of John (19:26), none of the men who had followed Jesus are mentioned as being present. They had fled in fear after the capture of Christ in the Garden of Gethsemane and after Peter's three-time denial of Christ.

But the women were there. They were risking their lives to be near the dying Christ, but they were there. It must have been the most agonizing moment in the life of Mary Magdalene. Here was the man who had recognized her as a person, who had released her from a life of captivity, and she could do nothing to help him. All the powers of the Roman state and the Jewish hierarchy were behind that crucifixion, and Mary Magdalene and the women with her were helpless to change the situation. It was a death of the spirit for them. They did not leave however. They hung on until the last. So it is not surprising that it was to Mary Magdalene and the women that Christ first appeared after his resurrection.

Now on the first day of the week Mary Magdalene came to the tomb early, while it was still dark, and saw that the stone had been taken away from the tomb. So she ran, and went to Simon Peter and the other disciple, the one whom Jesus loved, and said to them, "They have taken the Lord out of the tomb, and we do not know where they have laid him." . . .

But Mary stood weeping outside the tomb, and as she wept she stooped to look into the tomb; and she saw two angels in white, sitting where the body of Jesus had lain, one at the head and one at the feet. They said to her, "Woman, why are you weeping?" She said to them, "Because they have taken away my Lord, and I do not know where they have laid him." Saying this, she turned round and saw Jesus standing, but she did not know that it was Jesus. Jesus said to her, "Woman, why are you weeping? Whom do you seek?" Supposing him to be the gardener, she said to him, "Sir, if you have carried him away, tell me where you have laid him, and I will take him away." Jesus said to her, "Mary." She turned and said to him in Hebrew, "Rabboni!" (which means Teacher). Jesus said to her, "Do not hold me, for I have not yet ascended to the Father; but go to my brethren and say to them, I am ascending to my Father and your Father, to my God and your God." Mary Magdalene went and said to the disciples, "I have seen the Lord"; and she told them that he had said these things to her.—John 20:1–2, 11–18

The meeting of Christ and Mary Magdalene is an extraordinary recognition scene. It would appear that after his struggle with death, Jesus was not immediately recognizable. He was in his "resurrection body," but as soon as he communicated with Mary or with other disciples they knew who he was.

Mary tried to grasp Christ, to hang on to him, but this was not possible. Jesus is not just for one person but for everyone. She was passionately committed to him as a person, but he made her understand that he wanted her to carry out his work.

Mary Magdalene's characteristics and quality are made very clear by this encounter. First, she wanted to do all she could for her dead Lord by anointing his body with oil and bringing spices for a decent burial. Her preconceived mission was interrupted when it was found there was no body in the tomb. With great tenacity she tried to find the dead body, only to be confronted with a living Lord. She went to the heart of the matter; she knew who Jesus was. She could go beyond her own preconceptions to entertain a new reality.

Mary Magdalene has been variously portrayed as a repentant sinner, a converted hysteric, a prisoner of the flesh, and a devoted follower. What she has not been shown as is a woman who could see with clarity into the reality of things. She had seen much of the world and had suffered much. She had learned to separate the real from the unreal, and her allegiance was unswervingly to the real. She loved much and was ready to give everything in love. She dared to go to the tomb because she had found something more important than herself.

Women have always been the subject of fantasies and have often been beguiled by unreal pictures of themselves. They have accepted lesser goals rather than develop their real potential. Many times men are censured for this course, but seldom women.

Women can teach themselves to see clearly the reality of the situation and the reality of their own lives. This is the key to self-liberation.

Jesus saw Mary Magdalene as a person—a person who could and would creatively engage in his work of redemption. He chose her as the first person he revealed himself to after the resurrection. If Jesus' estimate of women was so high, should not ours be also?

Women's Response to Jesus During His Lifetime

Soon afterward he went on through cities and villages, preaching and bringing the good news of the kingdom of God. And the twelve were with him, and also some women who had been healed of evil spirits and infirmities . . . who provided for them out of their means.—Luke 8:1–3

There is no question from this reference and others that Jesus had women disciples, and that these women followed him in his preaching, teaching, and healing mission throughout Judea. This in itself is an amazing fact when we see it against the patriarchal society and prohibitions of his day.

> The significance of this phenomena of women following Jesus about, learning from and ministering to Him, can be properly appreciated when it is recalled that not only were women not to read or study the scriptures, but in the more observant settings they were not even to leave their household.[1]

Jesus' encouragement of women disciples was not only an acceptance of their grateful response to him after their healings or conversions but was an even more positive statement of his attitude toward women as equals of men and equally valuable as disciples. Peter Ketter puts this revolutionary idea in this way:

> But a fact much less noticed is that Jesus had a number of women also among this permanent following. This was *not* in accordance with the custom of teachers of the law. . . . Thus, Christ's toleration of women in his following was in itself a public proclamation of His differing estimate of women.[2]

In other words, Jesus did not have women as disciples by chance; he did it on purpose because he respected the abilities and powers of women. He knew his mission was not restricted but was for and by women and men.

Some names of these women followers have been recorded in the Gospels. There was Mary Magdalene; Joanna, the wife of Chuza, Herod's steward, and Susanna (Luke 8:3); Salome and Mary the mother of James and Joseph, and the mother of the sons of Zebedee (Matthew 27: 56); and Mary, the wife of Clopas, as well as Mary, his own mother (John 19:25). The presence of other women is mentioned only as "many women" or "many others."

Since it is evident that there were many women disciples of Jesus it may be asked why none were named among the twelve apostles. There are at least two major reasons for this. The first is very practical: In the Israel of Jesus' time women would not have been accepted as evangelists. The average Palestinian would not have listened to religion taught by a woman. It might have been even dangerous for a woman to attempt to preach and teach and spread the good news, since according to rabbinic teaching of the time women were not allowed to study religion. A first-century rabbi named Eliezar went so far as to say that the words of the Torah, the Hebrew scriptures, should be burned rather than entrusted to a woman. The climate of opinion would not accept a female religious teacher. Only a man was listened to in Judaism, which may be one reason why Jesus was born a male.

Later on, within the Christian community of the early church, women were accepted as prophets and teachers, but this was after the church had broken away from its predominantly Jewish character.

Another reason why the twelve apostles were men may have been that the new Israel was to follow the structure of the old twelve tribes of Israel. These twelve tribes were all masculine, the twelve sons of Jacob: Reuben, Simeon, Levi, Judah, Issachar, Zebulun, Joseph, Benjamin, Dan, Naphtali, Gad, and Asher. Therefore, the new Israel patterned on this prototype was also male. When we see how much the New Testament uses the prophecies and history of the Old Testament to fortify its position, this choice is not surprising. And in view of the prejudices of the time it was probably unavoidable.

One of the interesting things to note in the description of the women disciples is that they performed the role of deacons. "There were also women looking on from afar . . . who, when he was in Galilee, followed him, and ministered to him (Mark 15:40)." The Greek word for ministered to and provided for (Luke 8:3) is *diēkonoun,* the same word as deacon.*

The women remained at the crucial moment of the crucifixion, after the men had fled, as Mark 15:40, John 19:25, Matthew 27:55, and Luke 23:49 testify. These women, classified so gentle and timid, stayed by their savior to the end. They were faithful to death.

It was the women also who went to prepare the body of Jesus for burial on that first Easter Sunday. They brought spices and ointment so that the body of their dead lord might be decently buried. Mark records that it was Mary Magdalene and Mary, the mother of James, and Salome (16:1) who came; Matthew mentions Mary Magdalene and "the other Mary" (Matthew 28:1); while Luke says "they," later mentioning Mary Magdalene, Joanna, Mary, the mother of James, and the other women (Luke 24:10). These were the women who came to give last loving rites to the body.

But there was no body. Christ had risen. And it was to women that Jesus revealed the crucial fact of the resurrection. Not only did he reveal to them his rising from the dead, but he commanded them to be the bearers of this momentous news to the others.

---

* It is a bit ironic that it has taken the church almost two thousand years to catch up with the practice of Jesus. In 1970 the Protestant Episcopal Church in America voted to have women ordered deacons, and in the Diocese of Massachusetts the first woman, Elsa Walberg, was made a deacon in the Episcopal Church in Massachusetts in February 1972. (At the same time [in 1970] the Lutheran Church in America and the American Lutheran Church voted women into the ministry. Although the Roman Catholic Church and orthodox and conservative Judaism do not ordain women, reformed Judaism had its first woman rabbi in 1972, and the majority of Protestant sects now ordain women as ministers.)

> Now it was Mary Magdalene and Joanna and Mary the mother of James and the other women with them who told this to the apostles; but these words seemed to them an idle tale, and they did not believe them.—Luke 24:10–11

Swidler comments on the significance of this revelation.

> In typical male Palestinian style, the Eleven refused to believe the women since, according to Judaic law, women were not allowed to bear legal witness. As one learned in the Law, Jesus obviously was aware of this stricture. His first appearing and commissioning women to bear witness to the most important event of his career could not have been anything but deliberate: it was clearly a dramatic linking of a very clear rejection of the second-class status of women with the center of His gospel, His resurrection. The effort of Jesus to centrally connect these two points is so obvious that it is an overwhelming tribute to man's intellectual myopia not to have discerned it effectively in two thousand years.[3]

The record of Jesus' revelation of his resurrection to women first is an extraordinary witness. He knew and appreciated their true worth, their courage, and their faithfulness. They had witnessed to him, he would witness to them. He meant to turn their good Friday into an eternal Easter of acceptance and equality. The record of the Gospels on this is very positive, but instead of accepting the significance of the revelation, it has been relegated to an interesting narrative detail.

Women followed Jesus from the beginning of his ministry and were accepted as valued disciples. They stood by at his crucifixion and risked death to bury him properly. In all his encounters with them Jesus showed his understanding of their worth. In his resurrection he gave them the supreme accolade of being first witnesses to his triumph over death.

That the meaning of this shared moment of joy and glory should have been ignored over the ages is a tragedy in the life of the church and in the history of the world. Jesus chose women to be the witnesses to the event which gave supreme power to his life and teachings and which is the central motive for the founding of Christianity. Birth had been to a woman; rebirth was proclaimed to women. In this proclamation Jesus gave a responsibility to women to witness to him and the assurance that he loved, trusted, and had confidence in them to be first-class citizens in the new kingdom of the risen Lord.

14

Women in the Early Church

In the very beginning of the church, women played an important role. It was to the house of Mary, the mother of John Mark, that Peter fled when he was released from prison (Acts 12:12–17). And it was Lydia of Thyatira who was the first convert to Christianity in Europe.

Setting sail therefore from Troas, we made a direct voyage to Samothrace, and the following day to Neapolis, and from there to Philippi, which is the leading city of the district of Macedonia, and a Roman colony. We remained in this city some days; and on the sabbath day we went outside the gate to the riverside, where we supposed there was a place of prayer; and we sat down and spoke to the women who had come together. One who heard us was a woman named Lydia, from the city of Thyatira, a seller of purple goods, who was a worshiper of God. The Lord opened her heart to give heed to what was said by Paul. And when she was baptized, with her household, she besought us, saying, "If you have judged me to be faithful to the Lord, come to my house and stay." And she prevailed upon us.—Acts 16:11–15

Not only did Lydia become a convert, but she made her house the headquarters for the Christian mission in that area. The Christian church that was to grow up there came from these roots.

There were many other women who were prominent in the advance of the early church. There was Mary, the mother of John Mark, at whose house a prayer group met (Acts 12:12). There was Priscilla, who with her husband, Aquila, took Paul in when he was at Corinth (Acts 18:1–3). Phoebe, a deaconess of the church at Cenchreae, was a helper of Paul and many others in the Christian community (Romans 16:1–3). Mary, "who has worked hard among you (Rom. 16:6)," is commended by Paul. Chloe was also a leader in the Christian church at Corinth (1 Corinthians 1:11). Euodia and Syntyche are mentioned in the church at Philippi (Philippians 4:2). Timothy's grandmother, Lois, and his mother, Eunice, were influential Christians also (2 Timothy 1:5).

The activities of the early church were open to women. One at least was a deaconess (Romans 16:1). Women were included in prophesying, as Peter proclaimed in his great speech on the day of Pentecost recorded in Acts 2:17:

> And in the last days it shall be,
>   God declares,
> that I will pour out my Spirit upon
>   all flesh,
> and your sons and your daughters
>   shall prophesy.

The healing ministry of the church related to women also. One of the most dramatic healings of the New Testament was that of a woman, Tabitha, or Dorcas, of Joppa whom Peter raised from the dead (Acts 9:36–42). This disciple Tabitha was so full of acts of charity that widows witnessed to her good works, showing coats and garments she had made while she was with them, and the whole church rejoiced when she was returned to them.

The early Christian community often met in the houses of women, instead of in the temple. There were services in the house of Lydia (Acts 16:15) and of Prisca and Aquila (Paul speaks of "the church in their house" in Romans 16:3). Acts 12:12 testifies to Christian meetings in the house of Mary, the mother of John Mark. These early house churches were highly significant, because they changed the whole pattern of the role of women in religion. The change from the Jewish model of worship in the temple set up a whole new behavior for church. In the temple women were not counted as a quorum for a congregation. In the great temple at Jerusalem they were limited to the outer women's court and could not even enter the main temple. They were segregated from the men in synagogue meetings and could not read aloud or take any important role in the service. They were, in other words, second-class citizens. All this was changed, however, when they met in a household presided over by a woman, as Lydia's was. You could hardly exclude your hostess from participation in the service!

Women also shared in the hardships and persecution of the early church. They were taken to prison and to death along with the men and were as ready to suffer for their faith as the men were.

Anyone studying a calendar of saints or looking at the many paintings of canonized females must be amazed at the number of women martyrs who died for their Christian beliefs. Christian art abounds with women saints of the early church: Apollonia, a deaconess of the church of Alexandria in the third century; Catherine of Alexandria; St. Cecilia of Rome; St. Barbara with her tower; St. Dorothea of Cappadocia; St. Margaret of Antioch, patron saint of women in childbirth, also killed in the persecutions in the third century; and many others. These women were willing to die for Christian beliefs, because Christianity was the first religion which took women seriously—not as fertility goddesses or mother figures but as persons in their own right. In the beginning of its ministry, the early church, following the example of Jesus, gave women new dignity and new recognition as equals in the kingdom of God.

One of the great influences in the beginnings of the Christian church was the apostle Paul. Paul contributed in many ways to the idea of women as equals with men and as co-workers in the ongoing mission of the church. It is in his letter to the Galatians that we find his great affirmation of the position of women in Christianity: "There is neither Jew nor Greek, there is neither slave nor free, there is neither male nor female; for you are all one in Christ Jesus (Gal. 3:28)."

He also shared his ministry with women and acknowledged their help, as he says, "I commend to you our sister Phoebe, a deaconess of the church at Cenchreae, that you may receive her in the Lord as befits the saints, and help her in whatever she may require from you, for she has been a helper of many and of myself as well (Rom. 16:1–2)." He mentions Prisca and Aquila, "who risked their necks for my life (Rom. 16:3)," and Euodia and Syntyche, who "labored side by side with me in the gospel together with Clement and the rest of my fellow workers, whose names are in the book of life (Phil. 4:2–3)."

Paul knew in theory and in practice how important women were in the life of the new church. However, in certain practical matters of conduct he laid down precepts which have often been used to denigrate women. He spoke of the husband having rights over his wife's body and the wife over her husband's in 1 Corinthians 7:1–16. In 1 Corinthians 7:8–10 he gave his famous statement about it being better to marry than to burn with passion and opted for the single state; whereas in 1 Corinthians 7:38 he stated that he who marries his betrothed does well, but he who refrains from marriage does better. Paul commanded wives to be subject to their husbands in Ephesians 5:21–23 and Colossians 3:18–19, while in 1 Timothy 5:3–16 he was very strict regarding the conduct of young widows. He would have no woman's head uncovered in church (1 Corinthians 11:4–16), and he also forbade women to speak in church (1 Corinthians 14:33–35).

In view of his earlier statements and experience, why did Paul reduce the status of women? One answer is that he was governed by the traditions of his times. As one authority puts it: "As a product of the ancient Mediterranean world he held that the wife's role should be subordinate to that of her husband. Yet as one who attempted to imitate Jesus, he believed that men and women should have equal status." [1] In other words, the origin of his strictures on women was cultural, not theological.

Paul, as an apostle of the church in the gentile world, was also greatly concerned for the reputation of this new community. He was probably worried lest too much freedom for women would make it a laughingstock and turn possible converts away from an organization so different from the norm of the day.

Another reason for his prohibitions about entering into the new responsibilities of marriage may have been his feeling, shared by many in the early church, that the end of all things was close at hand, and to enter into a new relationship at this time was foolish. He expresses this in 1 Corinthians 7:29–31:

> I mean, brethren, the appointed time has grown very short; from now on, let those who have wives live as though they had none, and those who mourn as though they were not mourning, and those who rejoice as though they were not rejoicing, and those who buy as though they had no goods, and those who deal with the world as though they had no dealings with it. For the form of this world is passing away.

The urgency of this eschatology was later twisted out of context and Paul's statement was used against marriage in general.

Paul's antifeminism was deeply rooted in his Judaic past. From his training under the Pharisee Gamaliel, Paul received a rabbinical and Pharisaic bias against women. One who has studied Paul's life says, "Morally, Paul was an ascetic Jew." [2] This source gave him an intellectual and emotional background for feeling that women were inferior and dangerous. Before Paul became a follower of Christ he was Saul of Tarsus, persecuting Christians with all the strength of rabbinical conviction. It was not until his downfall on the Damascus road, as he was hurrying to imprison more Christians, that Paul had his vision of Jesus and his conversion to Christianity.

Paul became intellectually and spiritually a Christian, but emotionally and culturally he was still bound to Jewish tradition in regard to women.

Perhaps the most important thing to realize in connection with Paul's influential pronouncements about women is that he never witnessed Jesus' attitude toward them. As Elizabeth Farians puts it: "Paul's antifeminism is not in line with the wholesome attitude of Jesus towards women." [3]

Paul became an apostle after the death of Jesus. He did not see him in his encounters with women and did not hear how Jesus talked with them. Paul's knowledge of the gospel was intellectual and not existential. He had never experienced the example of Christ at work with people. The names of the women whom Christ encountered meant nothing to him; he could not really understand the revolutionary relationships that Jesus had with women. For Jesus, women were not theoretical beings who ought to be equal: they were living, breathing humans who were equals.

Perhaps if Paul had walked the roads of Galilee with Jesus, his ideas and actions would have been different. As it was, he left a legacy which has often been used against women and has been interpreted to make them second-class citizens. Ultimately, however, it is Jesus to whom we must look for a true estimate of women.

Jesus' Attitude Toward Women

"According to the received gospels, it is clear that Jesus was a feminist to a degree far beyond that of His fellows and followers." [1] This statement was made by an English historian in a book tracing the course of women in antiquity, not by a writer on religious equality or an advocate of women's liberation. It is an objective evaluation based on the study of history, not an argument in the service of a particular cause.

What is meant by the word feminist in this context? A feminist is a person who is in favor of equal rights for men and women. Usually a corollary to this is that a feminist is concerned with seeing women as human beings and as persons and is willing to contravene the prejudices of the day to do so.

Another writer, Sidney Callahan, puts it this way: "Christ himself treated women with a revolutionary equality and thereby constantly shocked the masculine prejudices of His disciples." [2] If Jesus surprised his male followers by his attitude, what was the effect on the women he encountered? John Snow, in a penetrating analysis of just how Jesus acted with women, writes:

> One has the feeling, when observing the responses to Jesus of the women in the Gospel stories, that Jesus was the first man in their experience who truly heeded them as persons, who would stop whatever he was doing to listen to them, to discuss seriously the

most profound issues of life with them and to understand the clearer vision of reality which they had.[3]

It was Jesus who proposed the Christian ideal of the individual allegiance to God regardless of sex, race, tribe, or nation. He emphasized the equality of all people in God's eyes. And he did not promote this ideal by precept only but by example as well. He went out of his way to show that he considered women as important as men. As our English historian again puts it:

> The Messiah was ever concerned with females as much as with men. No other Western prophet, seer or would be redeemer of humanity was so devoted to the feminine half of mankind. This cannot be too much emphasized because of the perversities of doctrine which ensued among male creatures professing not only to adore the First and Third Persons of the Trinity but also to imitate the example of the Second.[4]

Unfortunately, in the history of the Christian church women have often been assigned a secondary role. Such influential theologians as Augustine and Thomas Aquinas presented woman as a sexual snare and a being inferior to man. Aquinas went so far as to define women as defective males. These ideological positions, however, are far from the gospel as preached and practiced by Jesus. The true view of the situation is expressed by a young woman discovering the Christian message:

> Prejudice against women seemed as offensive to God as prejudice against blacks or Jews. In other words, the wrongs against women were just one more example of things that had to be righted in the name of justice. . . . I also got the very clear message that the responsibility for bringing the kingdom of God to earth was mine.[5]

The practice of Christians frequently falls short of this ideal. Dr. Mary Daly remarked, "It is painfully evident that there is a long road ahead. Christianity . . . has not yet faced its responsibility to exorcise the devil of sexual prejudice."[6]

The Christian religion, if it follows its founder, should make a radical witness in this area. It has at its root the person of Jesus of Nazareth who was crucified as a revolutionary. The early leaders of the church came from all strata of society and preached the revolutionary doctrine that all are equal in Christ. Women were prominent among its early leaders and devoted followers. If we ask that the church live up to its radical commitment, we are doing no more than Christ as the Head of this body expects us to do.

Many books have been written on areas of the church's concern for such minority groups as ghetto-dwellers, Blacks, the young, the poor, the psychologically or physically disadvantaged, but we have not seen women as belonging to a minority group or a deprived segment of society. Women numerically make up over 50 percent of the population, but in areas of policy and power they are in a minority. Their role and status within Christianity must be examined, and the church must go back to its roots in Jesus and both see and treat women as equals.

Women do not want to be regarded as superior or put on a pedestal like the statue of a saint in a dim niche. Women ask for what Jesus held out to them and gave them.

Jesus held out an invitation to women to become liberated from the hangups of second-class citizenship. He was very clear on a denial of seeing women primarily as a sex object: "You have heard that it was said, 'You shall not commit adultery.' But I say to you that every one who looks at a woman lustfully has already committed adultery with her in his heart (Matt. 5:27–28)." Betty Friedan has said, "The essence of the denigration of women is their definition as sex objects." [7] Jesus never treated women as sex objects, even a woman who appeared to be an obvious sex symbol, such as the woman of Samaria. He was always interested in the essential person regardless of the sex of that person. He discouraged exploitation of women in every way, whether as sex objects or as domestic servants.

Jesus did not define Christian service as domestic service by women but laid it out as an obligation on both sexes. There has been a mistaken idea that Christian service, in the case of women, is domestic service. Women have been called upon to fulfill themselves as Christians by serving others—their parents, husbands, children, grandchildren even. Surely this is too narrow an interpretation of Christian service. Strangely enough, the same "Christian service" does not apply to men. No, domestic service for women is an age-old pagan device and has nothing Christian about it. It may be a necessity to run a household, but the labor in it can be partially shared by all participants. Jesus did not put woman into the role of a domestic servant, as he makes quite clear in his treatment of Martha. He did not expect to be waited on hand and foot like some petty domestic tyrant. He preferred sharing in a one-to-one relationship with Mary.

There is a role of Christian service for women, but it is not confined to keeping a house. Christian service is the same for men and women, and it reaches out to the ends of the earth to minister to the deprived, the needy, the imprisoned, the sick, the hungry, and the stranger. Jesus said, "For I was hungry and you gave me food, I was thirsty and you gave me drink, I was a stranger and you welcomed me, I was naked and you clothed me, I was sick and you visited me, I was in prison and you came to me (Matt. 25:35-36)."

There is a great difference between a service of love and forced menial service. Service in Christ is a choice freely made. But if service is not a choice but an expected burden, then it can become a degradation and can separate a woman from her sense of self by turning her into a mere function.

For Jesus, women were not just functions as mother, wife, baby machine, nurse, housekeeper, cook, etc., but persons capable of making important decisions and commitments. In Luke 11:27-28 there is an interesting episode when Jesus was preaching: "As he said this, a woman in the crowd raised her voice and said to him, 'Blessed is the womb that bore you, and the breasts that you sucked!' But he said, 'Blessed rather are those who hear the word of God and keep it'."

This exchange could easily be interpreted as Jesus giving short shrift to flattery and pointing away from himself to the word of God. An alternate interpretation might be that Jesus was saying that the function an individual performs in one part of his or her life is not the thing which defines that person, but rather the choices that are made. The response a woman makes to the word of

God is what defines the character of the person, not whether she physically fills the role of motherhood.

The identification of a woman solely with the functions of wife and mother can eventually annihilate her sense of identity as a person under the duties of wifehood and motherhood. If she is only a function, she has been robbed of her God-given uniqueness as a person. In the same way, a man may be cast into the function of a breadwinner only and lose his birthright as a person.

Our society tends to type people very easily. We ask a woman about her children and a man about what he does. Both become less than persons in the exchange. Jesus never lost sight of the precious gift of individuality, the uniqueness of every person.

Jesus differed most from his society in his evaluation of women. He often made a radical break with the mores and expectations of his time. For example, he did not follow a double standard in dealing with sexual transgressions but considered that moral choice and responsibility should be dealt with equally for both sexes. This is evident in the story of the woman caught in the act of adultery recorded in John 8:1–11. Although this section is thought by some authorities to be a later addition to the fourth Gospel, it reflects early Christian thinking on what Jesus would do under the circumstances.

As the story goes, a woman caught in adultery is brought to Jesus by the Pharisees, and they ask how he would judge her. They have not brought her lover; he has evidently gotten off scot-free. The Pharisees set this up as a legal trap. If Jesus said the woman should be stoned for her crime according to Mosaic law, he would be going against Roman law and might get in trouble with the Roman rulers of Palestine. If he acquitted the woman, he would be contravening the law of Moses (Deuteronomy 22:22–29). Jesus did neither. He applied the whole question of transgression to her accusers: "Let him who is without sin among you be the first to throw a stone at her." He dealt with the question of sin across the board, and the same standards of righteousness applied to men as well as to women.

Jesus also protected the status of women in marriage. At that time in Israel there was the custom of unilateral divorce: a man could divorce his wife for practically any cause, but a woman had no rights of divorce. Jesus put both partners on an equal footing and protected the woman from possible repudiation when he said the binding quality of marriage applied equally to men.

And Pharisees came up and in order to test him asked, "Is it lawful for a man to divorce his wife?" He answered them, "What did Moses command you?" They said, "Moses allowed a man to write a certificate of divorce, and to put her away." But Jesus said to them, "For your hardness of heart he wrote you this commandment. But from the beginning of creation, 'God made them male and female.' 'For this reason a man shall leave his father and mother and be joined to his wife, and the two shall become one.' So they are no longer two but one. What therefore God has joined together, let not man put asunder."—Mark 10:2–9

In this way Jesus delivered women from the fear of unjust and capricious repudiation and made marriage an equal responsibility of men and women.

Besides meeting the innermost needs of women by his protection of their rights as individuals, Jesus also raised the self-image of women. What a person feels about herself is usually a result of what others have felt about her and how she has been treated by individuals and society. Jesus contributed to the self-esteem of women he met by treating them as important and significant in parables, in teaching, in action, and in his final revelation of his resurrection.

Jesus liberated women from the concepts of second-class citizenship so that they could become whole persons. He never made exceptions for the "weaker sex." He never excluded women from the demands of full personhood in the kingdom of God. Neither did he omit women from his promises at any time. He never considered them less than human in their vulnerabilities or their strengths. Jesus saw all people—men, women, and children—as children of God. He saw their faults and their virtues, their strivings and their failures. But he never sought to straitjacket one group with a label; he never typed people; he never responded to anyone just on the basis of sex, age, wealth, or race. He gathered together all those who were outcasts and alienated from society. He freed them from their alienation by his acceptance of them to full citizenship in his kingdom. Women were a significant number in the group of the rejected and alienated.

"Come to me, all who labor and are heavy-laden, and I will give you rest," Jesus said in Matthew 11:28. He could have been speaking of the burden of discrimination that women bear. As Simone de Beauvoir pointed out:

> It is, in point of fact, a difficult matter for men to realize the extreme importance of social discriminations which seem outwardly insignificant but which produce in women moral and intellectual effects so profound that they appear to spring from her original nature.[8]

In his contacts with women Jesus ignored the social discriminations of his time and effectively lifted this burden from women. In this way he was very much a social reformer regarding the attitudes and assumptions of people.

It has been said that Jesus is the example of the person we all should be. He himself said, "I am the way, and the truth, and the life; no one comes to the Father, but by me (John 14:6)." We are, therefore, asked to follow in his deliverance of both women and men from the burdens of sexual discrimination, economic favoritism, political elitism, legal partiality, role-playing, stereotyping, and all the other evils of a sexual caste system. Christ didn't ask men and women to give up their responsibilities. He asked them to take them on as persons, not as roles or predetermined functions.

In Christian doctrine it is held that Jesus was without sin. His actions, therefore, may be taken as models for us to follow. Jesus never treated one sex or the other as inferior beings or second-class citizens. If we are guilty of treating women or men in this way, we are going against the model he gave us. We are sinners, conscious or unconscious, in this form of discrimination. One of the strongest arguments for the true equality and real liberation of women is that Jesus was a fervent supporter of this policy.

If we wish to know what the Christian ideal of and for women is, we must look to the experiences and actions of Jesus Christ. When we look with eyes unblinded by prejudices or sentimentality, we see Jesus treating women with complete equality and confidence in their abilities. He demanded of them the conduct and commitment he asked of all his followers, and he gave them what he offered all humanity: the gift of eternal life.

Not only did he teach women, but he also learned from them. His relationships with women were reciprocal, not dependent or tyrannical. He recognized in each and every one a precious being in herself.

The example of Jesus in relationship to women is very clear, and the conclusion we may draw from it is unequivocal. He wills women to be liberated from the prejudices and burdens of society, to become whole persons. He encourages them to claim their birthright of freedom and to accept their true status as equals.

Any society which denies over half its members real participation in its benefits is on shaky ground, and Jesus had some words to say about a house divided against itself. Jesus stands as a great example and a righteous judge of our progress in the direction of equality. The record of his encounters with women gives us a very high standard to follow. His love and acceptance of women can be the inspiration for our actions in the world today. Jesus gives us a true estimate of the worth of each one as a person and an equal sharer in his kingdom.

Epilogue

The Revolution, Like the Kingdom of God, Is Within Us

The greatest block to women's achieving Jesus' ideal of equality for them has often been their own attitude about themselves. A woman who is a successful Wall Street stockbroker summed up the problem in this way:

> Getting men used to the idea of women leaders as decision makers isn't really the hard part. The really hard part is getting women to raise their *own* level of aspirations. In professional terms women must learn to think of themselves as executives, not "assistants to."
> . . . That's the most important and profound thing women's liberation can do, and until that happens women won't go through what reformed laws and practices have opened to them.[1]

Women have often become alienated from a sense of their true worth. They have lost their knowledge of self and self-worth. Their talents become lost in the shuffle of raising a family, and after ten or fifteen years of full-time work with a young family, the talents a woman originally possessed seem out of date. Women don't often have a chance to use their minds. Housewives are usually too busy or too tired to read or to pursue any intellectual project. After years of being a wife, mother, housekeeper, cook, chauffeur, and occasional volunteer worker, a woman loses her sense of personhood and uniqueness. None of the jobs a woman does in these years of child-raising are much valued by society, and they do not train or prepare her to engage in mature adult activity once the children are in school most of the day. As one woman said, who had completely lost her sense of purpose and identity as a person, "I'm a wife, mother, daughter, car pool driver and secretary for the P.T.A., but I don't know who I am!"

The culture in general offers a very limited definition of what it is to be a woman. A community college in New England offered the following criteria for its course called "On Being a Woman": individual instruction in skin care, manicure, pedicure, hair removal, hair care and styling, visual poise, body culture, makeup application and correction, voice and diction, and fashion coordination. Is this the pain and joy of being a woman? Can this definition of womanhood be offered to any mature person?

There are built-in limitations to being exclusively and entirely a housewife.

> The housewife who loses herself in things becomes dependent, like the things, upon the whole world: the linen is scorched, the roast burns, chinaware gets broken, these are absolute disasters, for when things are destroyed, they are gone forever. Permanence and security cannot possibly be obtained through them.[2]

Excessive concern with things, like Martha's, makes a woman's life too small. Housewifery by its nature is frustrating if it only resides in things—the house gets dirty, the meals are eaten, the clean clothes become soiled again.

When women seek their identity solely in a job, they are subject to the same limitations that men are. Who they are becomes equated with what they do. There is an idolatry present if we take models for ourselves below that of our creation in God's image. Women must be free to become whole as persons and to encompass more than occupational definitions.

If women are going to regain their sense of personhood, they must resist stereotyping into roles which limit their potential. Stereotypes of a class of people are often defenses to keep them in their place. As Shirley Chisholm observed:

The cheerful old darky on the plantation and the happy little home-maker are equally stereotypes drawn by prejudice. White America is beginning to be able to admit that it carries racial prejudice in its heart and that understanding marks the beginning of the end of racism. But prejudice against women is still acceptable because it is invisible.[3]

Women often accept men's stereotype of them as a sex object or a function. This is obviously a limitation on the person they could become. It does not grow from inside women but is imposed upon them. Women sometimes accept stereotypes and roles made up by a culture because it is easier to do so—the pains of conflict, search, and growth are avoided. This is fundamentally an Egyptian captivity. Although knowing who you are through your function offers the security of the fleshpots of Egypt, it is basically imprisonment. Women must go into the wilderness by breaking these stereotypes to find their own images and selfhood. Growth is often a bewildering and painful wandering in the wilderness, but it is necessary to reach the promised land of self-definition, self-realization, and true personhood.

There is a great temptation in any movement toward liberation to replace the image of the oppressed people by that of the oppressor. In the same way, there is a possibility of replacing the stereotyped image men have of women by woman's stereotyped image of male power: aggressive, bullying, self-determined, and bent exclusively on its own rights and privileges. This is not a true understanding of women or men as persons or human beings. It is just a reverse psychology which is equally as misguided as accepting outside categories and stereotyping.

In order to escape the bonds of a stereotype, women must evolve a sense of self and self-determination. In an article in *The New York Times Magazine* Dr. Joseph Adelson mentions the fact that to him the women's liberation movement has an overweening sense of self, as if women feel deprived and cheated. He says, "There is so much talk of self—of self-fulfillment, self-realization, self-determination—and so little of one's determination and responsibility to particular others—I don't mean mankind, I mean particular others." [4]

Let us analyze some of the sentiments behind this statement. Women seek a sense of self, because they lack a knowledge of selfhood. Men do not have to talk in terms of self, self-fulfillment, self-realization, etc., because this sense is already built into assumptions of their view of life. Their careers are seen as automatically self-serving, whereas women's are conceived of as serving others. In those rare cases where idealistic or altruistic young men seek to serve others, the "others" are not the "particular others" Dr. Adelson has reference to but are humanity at large. It is revealing that Dr. Adelson excludes serving mankind as a whole in women's service. This is, of course, a "masculine" activity of the idealistic variety.

The article mentions that women's liberation advocates appear to feel deprived and cheated, and, apparently, finds this odd. Women have been deprived and cheated. They are educated through grade school, high school, college, even post-graduate studies as equals of men in terms of courses and academic requirements. They pass the same examinations as male students, and the same assignments are required of them. Then, when they graduate, they find jobs of equal status with males are hard, if not impossible, to find. As Caroline Bird tells it in *Born Female*, if you went to Princeton, you were given an aptitude test on applying for a job; if you went to Vassar, a typing test. Even in the academic world, if a woman wants to teach, there are usually more openings for male professors in the higher levels of academia than for female ones. This is often as true at women's colleges as at universities or men's colleges.

After being taught to be a human being for twenty years, a woman is supposed to gracefully dwindle into being a wife, with a large emphasis on such menial tasks as housekeeping, cooking, cleaning, child care, and general domestic maintenance. Although marriage is supposed to be a partnership, in many cases it is hard for the male to see it as a 50-50 relationship. He wants to be head of his house, he wants his wife to match his ideals of womanhood, and he wants his home to conform to the stereotypes he has in mind. At social occasions he does not like to have his opinions contradicted by those of his wife. He does not want her to assert herself or her ideas too strongly, because this may cause friction or threaten other members of the group and, incidentally, his own authority. Small wonder then if women start losing a sense of self, learn to conform, and become superior domestic servants.

There is some necessity to sacrifice some of one's sense of self-hood when confronted with the multiple needs of infants and small children. Diapers must be washed, babies fed, children taken care of, house cleaned, etc., and often there isn't much time for any sense of self. Some of this load could be lightened, however, by help from the husband, and it often is, to everyone's satisfaction.

But society has oversold its education for women during this time when, if one has small children, service to particular others is necessary. If a woman has children when she is young, by the time they are partially independent and are going to school, she often feels she has lost her whole function. She has become so identified with the one dimension of motherhood that she has ceased to exist in any other dimension. Her sense of self has become extinguished, and she fills in her time with busywork, housework, unnecessary shopping, or multiple bridge games. She has been so channeled into the purpose of marriage and motherhood that any other goal in her life seems selfish or subversive.

This is one of the reasons why today's feminist leaders emphasize self-hood, self-fulfillment, and self-determination. It is a corrective to attitudes and education for self-evaluation on the part of women.

Many of the conflicts in marriage today stem from the fact that women's selves go underground and work their way out in trivial, hostile, or narcissistic expressions. The self exists in men and women, and it would seem best to recognize it and channel it in constructive ways.

Modern feminists often overcorrect prevailing stereotypes. They recognize the tyrannies of marriage as it now exists, and many are willing to renounce or drop out of marriage. They can see the self-lessness required in raising children, and they are willing to relinquish motherhood. Those who wish children but do not see becoming full-time slaves to child care want to change society and have child care centers so that mothers can work and continue in their careers or just work to support their families. Those who wish to raise children in a family situation often exchange work roles with the father so that he takes care of the children on a full- or part-time basis.

Modern science has created options so that today's woman is not dominated by her biological heritage of childbearing. She is free to choose to have children or not and is as free as a man to work at a career. The same selfhood and self-determination inherent in a man's role can be hers. At the same time it is easy to romanticize careers and freedom of choice. Men do not have the unlimited freedom of choice women often assign to them. They must take jobs they do not like because no others are available to them. Often their whole sense of identity is tied to their job. If they lose their job, their whole sense of self-worth and personhood crumbles. They must deal with bothersome details, boring routine, lack of advancement, favoritism, and all the other hazards of the business world. They constantly face the fear of failure. They must compete against cheating, lying, and all the many double-dealing devices the human being is capable of. They cannot be afraid of taking responsibility or retreat into a world where they cannot be attacked. Their performance is constantly being scrutinized, and they are constantly being judged on it. If women wish to enter this world, they must be subject to all these conditions and not plead special privileges on account of womanhood.

However, the business world is usually wastefully rigid in its requirements of employment. A nine-to-five work schedule is enforced, to the detriment of women who could get as much work done in a nine-to-three period and be home to greet their children after school. Employers who have tried this experiment have found that it worked, but the majority of companies exclude women who could and would work the shorter day. The result is either a vast waste of feminine talent and purpose or chaotic home schedules.

It is hard for a woman to retain a sense of self in contemporary society. She is either a consumer to be commercially exploited, a sex object to be sexually exploited, or a paid or unpaid worker to be economically exploited. A true sense of self for women can be the key to unlock realms of creativity and talent. A knowledge of the potentials of one's self as a person turns a woman from an object into a subject.

Basically, Christianity does not deal with objects but with subjects: that is, individuals with enough self-determination to make relevant choices. In Christ's dealing with women he consistently acknowledged this selfhood, this personhood, this identity that went beyond a role of domestic service. In his contacts with the crowds in Palestine he did not seek passive followers. He fished for people willing and able to make difficult choices, willing to be responsible for their lives. Jesus knew that a person can fulfill himself in service, but this service must be one which he or she has chosen, not one which has been thrust on the person or determined by someone else. He acknowledged the self in men and women and offered it a challenging mission.

Women must become revolutionaries in finding acceptable images of themselves and winning equality within the system. "You should remind women that perfect equality in their nature and dignity, and therefore in rights, is assured to them from the first page of the Sacred Scripture." The source for this quotation is the speech of Pope Paul VI in an Address to the Italian Women in Rome in 1965. The kind of radical equality that Jesus advocated means that woman is not a possession, not an object, not an extension of someone else, not a confirmation of someone else's status, not a function, and not a servant. The message to women comes loud and clear: don't sell out and don't sell yourself short, because it isn't only yourself you're selling, it's God's creation.

If we allow people to treat women as a category rather than acknowledging them as Christ did, as individual persons, we continue the stereotype.

Ultimately, the revolution is within each individual woman. If we allow society to present us with stereotypes to which we meekly conform, we are defeated as people. We must inform society rather than conform to it. "Do not be conformed to this world but be transformed by the renewal of your mind, that you may prove what is the will of God, what is good and acceptable and perfect (Rom. 12:2)."

Jesus made a complete break with the tradition of his day concerning women and showed that the world's standards were not his standards in this matter.

Women have conformed themselves to the world's estimate of themselves, because they have been taught conformity from the cradle. Conformity meant acceptance, popularity, identity with a group, and eventual success as a wife and mother. Conformity to others' standards has kept women from facing up to the challenge of growth, achievement, and personhood. However, it can be seen that conformity with the group, class, nation, or world's standards is often in conflict with conformity to the will of Jesus.

God wills women to be persons with all the difficulties and daring of true personhood. If we see this mandate as manifested in the character and behavior of Jesus of Nazareth, how can we refuse the challenge? The revolution, like the kingdom of heaven, is within us.

As long as women are seen as deficient males, acquiescent servants, or sex objects, there will be no change in the status of women. Until we follow the clues given by Christ in his relationship to women and become persons in our own right, the denigrating priorities of existence will remain. Our opportunity is to realize the revolution started by Jesus, to see that full personhood implies responsibility, decision, and sacrifice. If we ask for rights we must also accept responsibilities. But we must begin. The revolutionary doctrine of equal status has been proclaimed and practiced by Jesus and is ours to fulfill.

Notes

Chapter 2   Mary, the Mother of Jesus

1. Dorothy L. Sayers, *The Man Born to Be King* (New York: Harper & Bros., 1943), p. 40.

2. T. S. Eliot, *Collected Poems 1909–1962* (New York: Harcourt Brace Jovanovich, Inc., 1963). Used by permission of the publisher.

Chapter 8   The Samaritan Woman at the Well

1. George W. Cornell, *They Knew Jesus* (New York: William Morrow & Co., 1957), p. 109.

Chapter 9   Widows

1. *Interpreter's Dictionary of the Bible* (Nashville: Abingdon Press, 1962), III, 189.

Chapter 11   Mary of Bethany

1. Leonard Swidler, "Jesus Was a Feminist," *Catholic World*, Jan. 1971, p. 182.

2. *Interpreter's Dictionary of the Bible* (Nashville: Abingdon Press, 1962), III, 289.

Chapter 13   Women's Response to Jesus During His Lifetime

1. Leonard Swidler, "Jesus Was a Feminist," *Catholic World*, Jan. 1971, p. 180. Used by permission.

2. Peter Ketter, *Christ and Womankind* (Westminster, Md.: Newman Press, 1952), p. 273.

3. Swidler, op. cit., p. 179.

Chapter 14   Women in the Early Church

1. William A. Phipps, *Was Jesus Married?* (New York: Harper & Row, 1970), p. 114.

2. A. Powell Davies, *The First Christian* (New York: Farrar, Straus & Cudahy, 1957), p. 160.

3. Elizabeth Farians, "Women, Religion and Law," Congressional testimony, 1970–71, p. 3.

Chapter 15   Jesus' Attitude Toward Women

1. Charles Seltman, *Women in Antiquity* (2d ed., rev.; London: Pan Books Ltd., 1957), p. 148.

2. From *The Illusion of Eve* by Sidney Cornelia Callahan, © Sheed & Ward Inc., 1965, p. 37. Used by permission.

3. John H. Snow, *On Pilgrimage: Marriage in the '70s* (New York: Seabury Press, 1971), p. 136.

4. Seltman, op. cit., p. 149.

5. Callahan, op. cit.

6. Mary Daly, *The Church and the Second Sex* (New York: Harper & Row, 1968), p. 177.

7. Mary Lou Thompson, ed., *Voices of the New Feminism* (Boston: Beacon Press, 1970), p. 35.

8. Simone de Beauvoir, *The Second Sex*, trans. and ed. H. M. Parshley (New York: Alfred A. Knopf, 1953), p. xxvi.

Epilogue: The Revolution, Like the Kingdom of God, Is Within Us

1. Judith Hole and Ellen Levine, *Rebirth of Feminism* (New York: Quadrangle Books, 1971), p. 341.

2. Simone de Beauvoir, *The Second Sex*, trans. and ed. H. M. Parshley (New York: Alfred A. Knopf, 1953), p. 428.

3. Shirley Chisholm, *Unbought and Unbossed* (New York: Avon Books, 1971), p. 177.

4. Joseph Adelson, "Is Women's Lib a Passing Fad?", *The New York Times Magazine*, Mar. 19, 1972, p. 98.

Selected Bibliography

The Relationship of Jesus with Women

Blaine, Graham B., Jr. *Youth and the Hazards of Affluence.* New York: Harper & Row, 1966. This was a helpful reference for the chapter on the daughter of Jairus. The ambiguities and withdrawals of adolescence are well spelled out.

Brownrigg, Ronald. *Who's Who in the New Testament.* New York: Holt, Rinehart and Winston, 1971. An extremely attractive volume with beautiful photographs of Israel and artwork. The commentary is informative but lacks great depth.

Burkitt, F. C. "Mary Magdalene and Mary the Sister of Martha." *The Expository Times*, XLII (1930–31), 157–59. In this article dealing with the problems raised in biblical scholarship by the four different anointing stories, Burkitt holds that Mary of Bethany and Mary Magdalene are not the same person.

Cassels, Louis. *The Real Jesus: How He Lived and What He Taught.* Garden City, N.Y.: Doubleday, 1968. In this warm, readable book on the life of Jesus, Cassels makes several references to the relationship of women with Jesus.

Cornell, George W. *They Knew Jesus.* New York: William Morrow & Co., 1957. This is a helpful, well-researched book which explores in detail the characters of some of the men and women who met Jesus.

Corswant, Willy. *A Dictionary of Life in Bible Times,* ed. Arthur Heathcote. New York: Oxford University Press, 1960. A detailed reference for background material on customs in the time of Jesus.

Daniel-Rops, Henri. *Daily Life in the Time of Jesus.* Translated by Patrick O'Brian. New York: New American Library, 1964. This book supplies good material on the world of first-century Palestine.

Daube, David. "The Anointing at Bethany and Jesus' Burial." *Anglican Theological Review,* XXXII (1950), 186–99. An erudite exposition on the various meanings of the different anointing stories.

Davies, A. Powell. *The First Christian.* New York: Farrar, Straus, 1957. A scholarly book very rich in information about the first-century background of Paul's life and well-versed in biblical criticism, including revelations from the Dead Sea Scrolls.

Deen, Edith. *All of the Women of the Bible.* New York: Harper & Row, 1955. This excellent research book gives all the scriptural references for women in the Bible and a brief historical study on each one.

Eliot, T. S. *Collected Poems 1909–1962.* New York: Harcourt, Brace & World, Inc., 1963. This was used especially for the poem "The Journey of the Magi."

"Elsa Walberg Ordained Deacon." Newsletter of the Protestant Episcopal Diocese of Massachusetts, II (Apr. 1972). Brief article on the first woman to be ordained deacon in the diocese of Massachusetts.

Erskine, John. *The Human Life of Jesus.* New York: William Morrow & Co., 1945. This is an interesting book which speculates on the human interests of Jesus. It has some good material on the relationship of Jesus to women.

Harrison, Eveleen. *Little-Known Women of the Bible.* New York: Round Table Press, Inc., 1936. Although somewhat romantic and old-fashioned in approach, this book has some interesting information on some of the more obscure·women who met Jesus.

The Interpreter's Bible. Vols. VII, VIII. New York: Abingdon Press, 1952. A primary research tool for this book, with informed scholarly comment and stimulating exegesis on themes, these volumes had a quantity of good material on Jesus and women.

The Interpreter's Dictionary of the Bible. Vols. III, IV. New York: Abingdon Press, 1962. This is an excellent reference aid, with brief scholarly comment and solid bibliographical reference.

The Jerusalem Bible. Garden City, N.Y.: Doubleday & Co., Inc., 1966. This translation was especially helpful for the story of Esther.

Ketter, Peter. *Christ and Womankind.* Translated by Isabel McHugh.

Westminster, Md.: The Newman Press, 1952. Although somewhat dense in style and extended in scope, this book gives an interesting analysis of Christ's attitude toward women and upholds the view that Jesus was a feminist.

Lockyer, Herbert. *The Women of the Bible.* Grand Rapids, Mich.: Zondervan Publishing House, 1967. This thorough reference book gives name meanings and derivations and makes some appropriate comments on each of the women in the Bible.

Maertens, Thierry. *The Advancing Dignity of Women in the Bible.* Translated by Sandra Dibbs. DePere, Wisc.: St. Norbert Abbey Press, 1969. Maertens advocates the view that the position of women was progressively bettered from Old Testament times and found its greatest champion in Jesus.

Moore, Carey A. *Esther. (The Anchor Bible.)* Garden City, N.Y.: Doubleday & Co., 1971. A good, scholarly commentary on the book of Esther.

Morton, H. V. *Women of the Bible.* New York: Dodd, Mead & Co., 1941. Although occasionally sentimental in tone and fictional in approach, there are some helpful insights into women who met Jesus.

Phipps, William A. *Was Jesus Married?* New York: Harper & Row, 1970. A speculative and daring book which argues that Jesus probably was married due to the customs of the times, the witness of the warm relationship of Jesus with women and his conviction of their equality.

Rubenstein, Richard L. *My Brother Paul.* New York: Harper & Row, 1972. This is an interesting, profound vision of Paul interpreted in the light of Freudian analysis as well as biblical scholarship. Rubenstein feels that Paul's theology is basically an attempt at liberation from the finitude of the Law and death.

Sanders, J. N. "Those Whom Jesus Loved." *New Testament Studies,* I (1954–55), 29–41. A literate and probing article on the relationship of Jesus with Mary, Martha, and Lazarus of Bethany.

Sayers, Dorothy L. *The Man Born to Be King.* New York: Harper & Bros., 1943. A play which gives many shrewd insights into the character of women in the life of Jesus.

Schunemann, Imogene. "New Life for Widows." *Faith at Work,* LXXXV (Apr. 1972), 23. A brief article which looks at the contemporary role of widows.

Seltman, Charles. *Women in Antiquity.* 2d ed., rev.; London: Pan Books,

Ltd., 1957. A thorough, well-written, and witty account of the position of women in ancient history. Dr. Seltman comments on women in the first century and maintains that Jesus was a greater feminist than any of his fellows or followers.

Stendahl, Krister. *The Bible and the Role of Women.* Translated by Emilie Sander. Philadelphia: Fortress Press, 1966. In this scholarly pamphlet Dr. Stendahl, dean of Harvard Divinity School, argues that the Bible places no impediment to the full equality of women.

Swidler, Leonard. "Jesus Was a Feminist." *Catholic World,* Jan. 1971, pp. 177–83. A well-reasoned, scholarly article supporting the thesis that Jesus treated women as the equals of men. The author, an editor of the *Journal of Ecumenical Studies* and a member of the religion department at Temple University, gives cogent biblical examples to support his case.

———. "Jesus Was No Chauvinist." *Inside,* III (Jan. 1972), 15–16. A condensation of Swidler's earlier article cited above.

Women and Religion

Callahan, Sidney C. *The Illusion of Eve.* New York: Sheed & Ward, 1965. A brilliant, articulate book by a Roman Catholic woman who discusses the role of women in the world and in the church.

Daly, Mary. *The Church and the Second Sex.* New York: Harper & Row, 1968. This is a pioneer study on the Roman Catholic Church's discrimination against women in theological writing and in church policy and liturgy.

———. "Sisterhood and Sexism." Address given at the Women and Religion Symposium, Christ Church Parish Hall, Cambridge, Mass., Mar. 25, 1972. This is an advanced view on religious thinking given by an associate professor of theology at Boston College in which Dr. Daly argues against the patriarchal bias of Christianity and advocates the sharing community of sisterhood groups.

Doley, Sarah Bentley (ed.). *Women's Liberation and the Church.* New York: Association Press, 1970. An informed anthology on the question of women's liberation in Protestant and Catholic church policy. It also discusses the question of the ministry of women in the church.

Farians, Elizabeth. *Women, Religion and the Law.* Taken from testimony in 1970 in the U. S. Senate and in 1971 in the House on the Equal Rights for Men and Women amendment to the U. S. Constitution. Cogently written by Dr. Farians, head of the Ecumenical Task Force on Women and Religion of the National Organization for Women, this paper supports the view that Jesus was a feminist.

Ferguson, George. *Signs and Symbols in Christian Art.* New York: Oxford University Press, 1959. This was very helpful for female saints in the early church.

Harkness, Georgia. *Women in Church and Society.* Nashville: Abingdon Press, 1972. A fairly general treatment of the role of women in contemporary religious and secular organizations.

Reik, Theodor. *The Creation of Woman.* New York: George Braziller, Inc., 1960. In this book Reik tries to prove that Eve, far from coming from Adam's rib, was the original Mother Goddess.

Snow, John H. *On Pilgrimage: Marriage in the '70's.* New York: Seabury Press, 1971. An excellent and informed study of marriage and its problems in contemporary society, this book is particularly searching in its approach to the relation of men and women and woman's quest for identity.

Wolf, William J. "Should Women be Ordained? Yes." *The Episcopalian,* Feb. 1972, p. 9. In this article, Dr. Wolf, a professor at The Episcopal Theological School, concludes that "whoever opposes the ordination of women opposes the gospel of Jesus Christ and disqualifies half the human race."

The Liberation of Women

Adelson, Joseph. "Is Women's Lib a Passing Fad?" *The New York Times Magazine,* Mar. 19, 1972, pp. 26–27, 93–98. Dr. Adelson holds that women's lib has an overweening sense of self and a feeling of being deprived and cheated. His tone is logical—and condescending.

Amundsen, Kirsten. *The Silenced Majority: Women and American Democracy.* Englewood Cliffs, N.J.: Prentice-Hall, 1971. A study on the paucity of political power and effectiveness of women.

Andreas, Carol. *Sex and Caste in America.* Englewood Cliffs, N.J.: Prentice-Hall, 1971. A sociological analysis of discrimination against women in America, with adequate documentation of the author's contention.

Babcox, Deborah and Belkin, Margaret. *Liberation Now.* New York: Dell Publishing Co., 1971. Organized by a group of women editors, this is a challenging book which reflects many different views within the women's liberation movement.

Beauvoir, Simone de. *The Second Sex.* Translated and edited by H. M.

Parshley. New York: Alfred A. Knopf, 1953. A profound, seminal examination of what it means to be a woman, by a great literary figure. The references to psychology, medicine, religion, and literature are erudite and challenging.

Bird, Caroline. *Born Female: The High Cost of Keeping Women Down.* New York: David McKay, 1968. One of the first studies on economic discrimination against women, this is well documented and far reaching in its research.

Calhoun, Susan Kennedy. "Women in the Professional School." *Yale Alumni Magazine,* XXXIII (Apr. 1970), pp. 43–55.

Chisholm, Shirley. *Unbought and Unbossed.* New York: Avon Books, 1971. This is the autobiography of Shirley Chisholm; well written and convincing. It says a great deal about the black woman in America, her deprivations and her need for liberation.

Cudlipp, Edythe. *Understanding Women's Liberation.* New York: Paperback Library, 1971. Although it contains much interesting information and is helpful in giving names and addresses of women's liberation groups and publications, this is a somewhat superficial book, poorly organized and occasionally contradictory in its statements.

Deutsch, Helene. *The Psychology of Women.* New York: Grune & Stratton, 1945, Vol. II. Although she overemphasizes certain culturally induced elements in women's psychological make-up, some interesting observations about women are presented in this book.

Didion, Joan. "The Women's Movement." *The New York Times Book Review,* July 30, 1972, pp. 1–2, 14. A brilliant analysis of the women's liberation movement, pointing out its weaknesses as well as its strengths, with an excellent brief bibliography.

Ellmann, Mary. *Thinking About Women.* New York: Harcourt, Brace Jovanovich, 1968. A literate essay on the discrimination against women writers and women in literature. The author gives very good examples and writes with wit and authority.

Epstein, Cynthia Fuchs and Goode, William J. (eds.). *The Other Half: Roads to Women's Equality.* Englewood Cliffs, N.J.: Prentice-Hall, 1971. This book includes essays on the position of women today, how women are employed, and feminist movements in the United States. It has some good material but is rather bland and obvious.

Ermarth, Margaret S. *Adam's Fractured Rib.* Philadelphia: Fortress Press,

1970. This book deals with the condition of women in the church and is generally critical of church polity and policy.

Farber, Seymour M. and Wilson, Roger H. (eds.) *The Potential of Woman*. New York: McGraw-Hill, 1963. A transcript of numerous conferences on the position of women in our society, with many profound biological, anthropological, psychological, and humanistic observations. Both men and women participated on the panels, one of the best contributions being made by Marya Mannes.

Firestone, Shulamith. *The Dialectic of Sex: The Case for Feminist Revolution*. New York: Bantam Books, 1971. This is a passionate book but often with more passion than sense. The author's view seems biased by unhappy experiences which she holds to be universal. Her blueprint for the future appears to be utopian and inhuman.

Freire, Paulo. *Pedagogy of the Oppressed*. Translated by Myra Bergman Ramos. New York: Herder & Herder, 1970. The author is a Brazilian educator, a political exile from Brazilian military dictatorship, and presently Special Consultant to the Office of Education of the World Council of Churches in Geneva. This is a brilliant book which defines the meaning of an oppressed class and suggests steps to remedy such oppression. It can be and has been applied to the condition of women in our time.

Friedan, Betty. *The Feminine Mystique*. New York: Norton Co., 1963. The first book of the new feminist wave which reveals in detail some of the manipulations of women into an exclusively housewife role. This book was written by the founder of the National Organization of Women, who feels that women are not treated as persons or equals in our society.

Golden, Janet. *The Quite Possible She*. New York: Herder & Herder, 1966. A book on the development of woman from a Christian viewpoint.

Gornick, Vivian and Moran, Barbara K. *Woman in Sexist Society*. New York: Basic Books, 1971. This is an anthology of some thoughtful feminist writing. It reveals some of the discriminations women encounter when they attempt to take a job in a man's world.

Greer, Germaine. *The Female Eunuch*. New York: McGraw-Hill, 1971. Erudite and witty, this book promises more than it delivers.

Hole, Judith and Levine, Ellen. *Rebirth of Feminism*. New York: Quadrangle Books, 1971. An excellent resource book, drawing heavily on factual material, statistics, and interviews. It is well organized and authoritative.

Lifton, Robert J. (ed.). *The Woman in America*. Boston: Houghton

Mifflin, 1965. This anthology includes essays by Erik Erikson, Diana Trilling, David Riesman, Alice S. Rossi, Esther Peterson, and others. Although occasionally dated, it is an interesting exploration into the state of womanhood in America. The essays by Rossi and Peterson are of special value in their documentation of the economic deprivation of women.

Miller, Casey and Swift, Kate. "One Small Step for Genkind." *The New York Times Magazine*, Apr. 16, 1972, pp. 36, 99–101, 106. This is an intelligent article which discusses the patriarchal bias of semantics and the challenges to the system, particularly in theological language alternatives.

Millett, Kate. *Sexual Politics.* New York: Doubleday & Co., 1970. Originally written as a doctoral thesis, this book is occasionally rather dense reading. It deals with the suppression and stereotyping of women by political parties, as in Nazi Germany. Dr. Millett quotes from a variety of sources derogatory to women.

Morgan, Elaine. *The Descent of Woman.* New York: Stein & Day, 1972. An intelligent, witty book, written by an Oxford-trained writer of brilliance and imagination, which examines the origin of the species through the eyes of the female sex rather than the presuppositions of androcentric writers such as Morris and Ardrey. The book is well researched and a delight to read.

Morgan, Robin (ed.). *Sisterhood Is Powerful.* New York: Random House, 1970. An inclusive, honest anthology of the difficulties women of all types —Mexican-Americans, Blacks, radicals, middle-aged housewives, career women, etc.—face in their quest to be effective persons. Some of the descriptions sound pretty far out, others very close to home.

MS. magazine. A newly published magazine which examines many of the concerns of the women's liberation movement.

Sayers, Dorothy. *Unpopular Opinions.* New York: Harcourt, Brace & Co., 1947. In two essays, "Are Women Human?" and "The Human Not-quite-human," Dorothy Sayers makes a strong case for the humanity of the female sex and also points out that Jesus always treated women as persons, rather than as a class.

Thompson, Mary Lou (ed.). *Voices of the New Feminism.* Boston: Beacon Press, 1970. A fine anthology of articles by noted female writers in a variety of spheres, including religion, politics, and economics.